The
NEW YORK DIRECTORY
for 1786

Illustrated with a Plan of the City

Also Changes in the Names of Streets

by
David Franks

PREFACED
by a General Description by
NOAH WEBSTER

Originally Published by
H. J. Sachs & Company in 1905

HERITAGE BOOKS
2012

HERITAGE BOOKS

AN IMPRINT OF HERITAGE BOOKS, INC.

Books, CDs, and more—Worldwide

For our listing of thousands of titles see our website
at
www.HeritageBooks.com

A Facsimile Reprint
Published 2012 by
HERITAGE BOOKS, INC.
Publishing Division
100 Railroad Ave. #104
Westminster, Maryland 21157

Originally published:

H. J. Sachs & Company
Real Estate
8 West 22nd Street
New York
1905

International Standard Book Numbers
Paperbound: 978-0-7884-0810-6
Clothbound: 978-0-7884-9318-8

THE

NEW YORK DIRECTORY

FOR

1786.

ADVERTISEMENT.

THE only perfect original copy which has been found of this Directory, after considerable inquiry by the Publisher, is in the Library of the NEW YORK HISTORICAL SOCIETY. The alphabetical arrangement contains 855 names, to which may be added 71 names on pages 52, 62, and 80, that do not appear in their regular place; making together a total of 926 names in this work. The population of the city when this Directory originally appeared, was 23,614; the present population is 515,394.

In this edition the orthography, punctuation and arrangement of the original have been strictly copied.

A key to the changes in the names of the streets may be found on the next page.

The map of the city which accompanies this publication, is copied from one appended to a New York Directory for 1789.

Key to the Changes in the Names of Streets,

SO FAR AS ASCERTAINED.

———•❖•———

FORMERLY CALLED	NOW CALLED
Chatham Row,	*Park Row.*
Crown st.	*Liberty st.*
Dock st.	*Pearl st. between Broad st. and Hanover Sq.*
Duke st.	*South William st.*
Dyes st.	*Dey st.*
Fair st.	*Fulton st. bet. B.way and Cliff st.*
Garden st.	*Exchange Place.*
George st.	*Spruce st.*
Golden Hill,	*John st. between William and Pearl*
King George st.	*William st. bet. Frankfort and Pearl*
King st.	*Pine st.*
Little Dock st.	*South st. bet. Whitehall and Old Slip*
Little Queen st.	*Cedar st.*
Magazine st.	*Part of Pearl st.*
Mill st.	*Part of South William st.*
Partition st.	*Fulton st. bet. B.way and the N. R.*
Princess st.	*Beaver st. bet. Broad and William*
Queen st.	*Pearl st. bet. Wall st. and B.way.*
Robinson st.	*Park Place.*
St. James st.	*James st.*
Smith st.	*William st. between Old Slip and Liberty st.*

THE

NEW-YORK DIRECTORY,

CONTAINING,

A Valuable and well Calculated ALMANACK ;— Tables of the different COINS, suitable for any State, and digested in such order, as to render an Exchange between any of the United States plain and easy.

LIKEWISE,

1. The names of all the Citizens, their occupations and places of abode.
2. The members in Congress, from what State, and where residing.
3. Grand departments of the United States for adjusting public accounts, and by whom conducted.
4. Members in Senate and Assembly, from what county, and where residing.
5. Judges, Aldermen, and other civil officers, with their places of abode.
6. Public state-officers, and by whom kept.
7. Counsellors at law, and where residing.
8. Ministers of the gospel, where residing and of what Church.
9. Physicians, Surgeons, and their places of abode.
10. President, Directors, days, and hours of business at the Bank.
11. Professors, &c. of the university of Columbia college.
12. Rates of postage, as by law established.
13. Arrivals and departures of the mails at the Post-Office.

BY DAVID FRANKS.

NEW-YORK:

Printed by SHEPARD KOLLOCK, corner of Wall and Water Streets, M, DCC, LXXX, VI.

REPUBLISHED BY JOHN DOGGETT Jr., 59 LIBERTY STREET, NEW YORK, 1851.

JANUARY begins on SUNDAY hath XXXI Days.

First Quarter the 7th day, 7 in the Morning.
Full Moon the 14th day, 7 in the Morning.
Laft Quarter the 22d day, 6 in the Morning.
New Moon the 29th day, 10 in the Afternoon.

D. M.	W. days	Festivals, Remarkable Days, &c.	Sun rifes H.M	Sun rifes H.M	Moon fets H. M.	M. age	High Water H. M.
1	Sund	Circumcifion.	7 23	4 37	5 58	2	9 56
2	Mon	Can.at Trenton	7 23	4 37	7 10	3	10 52
3	Tuef	Bat.of Princeton	7 22	4 38	8 26	4	11 51
4	Wed		7 22	4 38	9 36	5	Aft. 44
5	Thur		7 22	4 38	10 51	6	1 34
6	Frid	Epiphany.	7 21	4 39	11 58	7	2 24
7	Satu		7 21	4 39	Morn.	8	3 18
8	Sun	1 Sund. paft Epip.	7 20	4 40	1 6	9	4 10
9	Mon		7 19	4 41	2 26	10	5 3
10	Tuef		7 19	4 41	3 36	11	5 53
11	Wed		7 18	4 42	4 47	12	6 46
12	Thur		7 18	4 42	5 46	13	7 37
13	Frid	Days 9 hours 26m.	7 17	4 43	6 42	14	8 30
14	Satu		7 16	4 44	Rifes	15	9 15
15	Sund	2 Sund. paft Epip.	7 15	4 45	6 10	16	9 50
16	Mon		7 14	4 46	7 18	17	10 38
17	Tuef		7 13	4 47	8 21	18	11 21
18	Wed		7 12	4 48	9 24	19	Morn.
19	Thur		7 12	4 48	10 19	20	0 56
20	Frid	Prelim. Art. 1783.	7 11	4 49	11 19	21	1 34
21	Satu		7 10	4 50	Morn.	22	2 28
22	Sund	3 Sund. paft Epip.	7 9	4 51	0 19	23	3 16
23	Mon		7 8	4 52	1 19	24	4 5
24	Tuef	Days 9h. 46m,	7 7	4 53	2 20	25	4 52
25	Wed	Conver. of St.Paul	7 6	4 54	3 24	26	5 40
26	Thur		7 5	4 55	4 24	27	6 32
27	Frid		7 4	4 56	5 24	28	7 24
28	Satu		7 3	4 57	6 24	29	8 16
29	Sund	4 Sund. paft Epip.	7 2	4 58	Sets	30	9 8
30	Mon		7 1	4 59	5 58	1	9 56
31	Tuef	Days 10h. 0m.	7 0	5 0	7 11	2	10 4

1*   A 2

FEBRUARY begins on WEDNESDAY, XXVIII Days.

Firſt Quarter the 5th day, 3 in the Afternoon.
Full Moon the 12th day, at midnight.
Laſt Quarter the 21ſt day, 3 in the morning.
New Moon the 28th day, 10 in the morning.

D. M.	W. days	Feſtivals, Remarkable Days, &c.	Sun riſes H.M	Sun ſets. H M	Moon ſets. H. M.	M. age	High Water H. M.
1	Wed		6 59	5 1	8 26	3	11 32
2	Thur	Purifica. V. Mary.	6 58	5 2	9 38	4	Aft. 21
3	Frid		6 57	5 3	10 48	5	1 12
4	Satu	Days 10h. 8m.	6 56	5 4	11 58	6	2 4
5	Sund	5 Sund. p. Epip.	6 54	5 6	Morn.	7	2 53
6	Mon	French Alli. 1778.	6 53	5 7	1 20	8	3 44
7	Tueſ		6 52	5 8	2 30	9	4 46
8	Wed		6 51	5 9	3 30	10	5 35
9	Thur	Days 10h. 14m.	6 50	5 10	4 26	11	6 27
10	Frid		6 48	5 12	5 18	12	7 14
11	Satu		6 47	5 13	5 54	13	8 2
12	Sund	Septuag. Sund.	6 46	5 14	Rises.	14	8 50
13	Mon		6 45	5 15	6 2	15	9 37
14	Tueſ	Valentine.	6 44	5 16	7 8	16	10 26
15	Wed		6 42	5 18	8 8	17	11 14
16	Thur		6 41	5 19	9 8	18	11 58
17	Frid	Days 10h. 36m.	6 40	5 20	10 8	19	Morn.
18	Satu		6 39	5 21	11 9	20	1 24
19	Sund	Sex ageſi. Sund.	6 38	5 22	Morn.	21	2 10
20	Mon		6 37	5 23	0 10	22	2 54
21	Tueſ		6 35	5 25	1 10	23	3 48
22	Wed		6 34	5 26	2 10	24	4 36
23	Thur		6 33	5 27	3 4	25	5 24
24	Frid	St. Matthias.	6 32	5 28	3 51	26	6 12
25	Satu	Days 10h. 59m.	6 31	5 29	4 30	27	7 0
26	Sund	Quinquæg. Sund.	6 29	5 31	5 6	28	7 53
27	Mon		6 28	5 32	5 36	29	8 40
28	Tueſ		6 27	5 33	Sets.	1	9 24

The Planet *Venus* will be Morning Star till March 22d, then Evening Star till the Year's end.

MARCH begins on WEDNESDAY, hath XXXI Days.

First Quarter the 6th day, at Midnight.
Full Moon the 14th day, 5 in the Afternoon.
Last Quarter the 22d day, 9 in the Afternoon.
New Moon the 29th day, 7 in the Afernoon.

D.M.	W. days	Festivals, Remarkable Days, &c.	Sun rises H.M	Sun sets HM	Moon sets H.M.	M. age	High Water H.M.
1	Wed	St. David, and Ash	6 25	5 35	7 16	2	10 16
2	Thur	Wednesday.	6 24	5 36	8 34	3	11 11
3	Frid		6 22	5 38	9 54	4	Aft. 8
4	Satu	Days 11h. 16m.	6 21	5 39	11 0	5	1 1
5	Sund	1 Sund. in Lent.	6 19	5 41	*Morn.*	6	1 52
6	Mon		6 18	5 42	0 24	7	2 44
7	Tues		6 17	5 43	1 33	8	3 30
8	Wed		6 15	5 45	2 30	9	4 20
9	Thur	Days increase 27m	6 14	5 46	3 17	10	5 9
10	Frid		6 13	5 47	3 57	11	5 53
11	Satu	G. Wash. born 32.	6 11	5 49	4 30	12	6 40
12	Sund	2 Sund. in Lent.	6 10	5 50	4 58	13	7 32
13	Mon		6 9	5 51	5 21	14	8 20
14	Tues		6 7	5 53	*Rises.*	15	9 8
15	Wed	.	6 6	5 54	7 0	16	9 56
16	Thur		6 5	5 55	8 0	17	10 40
17	Frid	St. Patrick.	6 3	5 57	9 1	18	11 24
18	Satu		6 2	5 58	10 2	19	*Morn.*
19	Sund	3 Sund. in Lent.	6 0	6 0	11 3	20	0 8
20	Mon		5 59	6 1	*Morn*	21	0 54
21	Tues	Day & Night equal	5 58	6 2	0 C	22	1 40
22	Wed		5 57	6 3	1 4	23	2 26
23	Thur		5 55	6 5	1 56	24	3 16
24	Frid		5 54	6 6	2 36	25	4 6
25	Satu		5 52	6 8	3 16	26	5 0
26	Sund	4 Sund. in Lent.	5 51	6 9	3 53	27	5 50
27	Mon		5 50	6 10	4 25	28	6 44
28	Tues		5 49	6 11	4 48	29	7 48
29	Wed		5 48	6 12	*Sets.*	30	8 42
30	Thur	Days 12h. 24m.	5 46	6 14	7 30	1	9 42
31	Frid		5 45	6 15	8 50	2	10 40

APRIL begins on SATURDAY, hath XXX Days.

First Quarter, the 5th day, 11 in the morning.
Full Moon, the 13th day, 10 in the morning.
Last Quarter, the 21ft day, 11 in the Morning.
New Moon, the 28th day, 3 in the Morning.

D. M.	W. days	Festivals, Remarkable Days, &c.	Sun rises H M	Sun fets. H M	Moon fets. H. M.	Age	High Water H. M.
1	Satu	Days 12th. 32m.	5 44	6 16	10 4	3	11 37
2	Sund	5 Sund. in Lent.	5 43	6 17	11 20	4	Aft. 34
3	Mon		5 42	6 18	Morn.	5	1 24
4	Tuef		5 40	6 20	0 26	6	2 10
5	Wed		5 39	6 21	1 24	7	3 0
6	Thur		5 38	6 22	2 9	8	3 50
7	Frid		5 37	6 23	2 36	9	4 42
8	Satu		5 35	6 25	3 7	10	5 34
9	Sund	Palm Sunday.	5 34	6 26	3 32	11	6 19
10	Mon		5 33	6 27	3 58	12	7 8
11	Tuef		5 32	6 28	4 16	13	7 53
12	Wed	Days 12h. 54m.	5 30	6 30	4 38	14	8 42
13	Thur		5 29	6 31	Rifes.	15	9 27
14	Frid	Good Friday.	5 28	6 32	8 0	16	10 12
15	Satu		5 26	6 34	9 0	17	10 57
16	Sund	Easter Sunday.	5 25	6 35	10 0	18	11 42
17	Mon		5 24	6 36	11 0	19	Morn.
18	Tuef		5 23	6 37	11 58	20	0 37
19	Wed	Bat. of Lexing. 75.	5 22	6 38	Morn.	21	1 27
20	Thur		5 20	6 40	0 47	22	2 21
21	Frid	Days 13h. 22m.	5 19	6 41	1 20	23	3 11
22	Satu		5 18	6 42	1 52	24	4 55
23	Sund	Sunday past East.	5 17	6 43	2 22	25	5 3
24	Mon		5 16	6 44	2 49	26	5 57
25	Tuef		5 15	6 45	3 20	27	6 51
26	Wed		5 13	6 47	3 42	28	7 49
27	Thur		5 12	6 48	4 2	29	8 43
28	Frid	Days 13h. 38m.	5 11	6 49	fets.	1	9 37
29	Satu		5 10	6 50	9 6	2	10 37
30	Sund	2 Sund. past. East.	5 8	6 52	10 17	3	11 31

MAY begins on MONDAY, hath XXXI Days.

First Quarter the 4th day, 11 in the Afternoon.
Full Moon the 13th day, 2 in the Morning.
Last Quarter the 20th day 9 in the Afternoon.
New Moon the 27th day, 11 in the Morning.

D. M.	W. days	Festivals, Remarkable Days, &c.	Sun rifes H.M	Sun fets. H M	Moon fets. H. M.	M. age	High Water H. M.
1	Mon		5 7	6 53	11 16	4	Aft. 22
2	Tuef		5 6	6 54	Morn.	5	1 12
3	Wed	Days 13 h 50m.	5 5	6 55	0 2	6	2 1
4	Thur		5 3	6 57	0 43	7	2 51
5	Frid		5 2	6 58	1 14	8	3 37
6	Satu		5 1	6 59	1 44	9	4 27
7	Sund	3 Sund. p. Eaft.	5 0	7 0	2 10	10	5 17
8	Mon		4 59	7 1	2 33	11	6 07
9	Tuef		4 58	7 2	2 51	12	6 52
10	Wed	Cong. met 1775.	4 57	7 3	3 10	13	7 32
11	Thur		4 56	7 4	3 34	14	8 17
12	Frid	Char. fur. 1780.	4 56	7 4	4 1	15	6 6
13	Satu	Days 14h. 10m.	4 55	7 5	Rifes	16	9 51
14	Sund	4 Sund. p. Eaft.	4 54	7 6	9 6	17	10 36
15	Mon		4 53	7 7	9 58	18	11 21
16	Tue		4 52	7 8	10 32	19	Morn.
17	Wed		4 51	7 9	11 24	20	0 10
18	Thur		4 50	7 10	11 56	21	1 2
19	Frid	Days 14h. 24m.	4 49	7 11	Morn.	22	1 50
20	Satu		4 48	7 12	0 22	23	2 46
21	Sund	Rogation Sund.	4 47	7 13	0 49	24	3 42
22	Mon		4 46	7 14	1 14	25	4 35
23	Tuef		4 45	7 15	1 44	26	5 30
24	Wed		4 44	7 16	2 11	27	6 26
25	Thur	Afcenfion Day.	4 44	7 16	2 43	28	7 20
26	Frid		4 43	7 17	3 21	29	8 14
27	Satu	Days 14h. 34m.	4 43	7 17	Sets.	1	9 8
28	Sund	Sund. aft. Afcen.	4 42	7 18	9 0	2	9 58
29	Mon		4 41	7 19	9 50	3	10 52
30	Tuef		4 41	7 19	10 33	4	11 42
31	Wed		4 40	7 20	11 14	5	Aft. 31

JUNE begins on THURSDAY, hath XXX days.

First Quarter 3d day, 2 in the Afternoon.
Full Moon the 11th day 5 in the Afternoon.
Last Quarter the 19th day, 4 in the Morning.
New Moon the 25th day, 7 in the Afternoon.

D. M.	W. days	Festivals, Remarkable Days, &c.	Sun rifes H M	Sun fets H M	Moon fets. H. M.	Moon's Age	High Water H. M.
1	Thur	Bofton p.fhut 1774	4 40	7 20	11 38	6	1 3
2	Frid		4 39	7 21	Morn.	7	2 16
3	Satu	Days 14h. 42.m.	4 39	7 21	0 8	8	3 6
4	Sund	Whifunday.	4 38	7 22	0 28	9	3 56
5	Mon		4 38	7 22	0 54	10	4 46
6	Tuef		4 38	7 22	1 12	11	5 32
7	Wed		4 37	7 23	1 56	12	6 17
8	Thur		4 37	7 23	2 16	13	7 4
9	Frid		4 37	7 23	3 1	14	7 46
10	Satu		4 36	7 24	3 58	15	8 32
11	Sund	Trinity Sunday, &	4 36	7 24	Rifes.	16	9 17
12	Mon	St. Barnabas	4 36	7 24	8 38	17	10 11
13	Tuef		4 36	7 24	9 14	18	10 59
14	Wed		4 35	7 25	9 48	19	11 52
15	Thur	Days 14h. 54m.	4 35	7 25	10 20	20	Morn.
16	Frid		4 35	7 25	10 49	21	0 40
17	Satu	Bat of B. Hill, 75.	4 35	7 25	11 14	22	1 35
18	Sund	1 Sund.paft. Trini.	4 35	7 25	11 41	23	2 33
19	Mon	Britifh evacua.Phi-	4 35	7 25	Morn.	24	3 23
20	Tuef	ladelphia, 1778.	4 35	7 25	0 8	25	4 17
21	Wed	Longest day.	4 35	7 25	0 33	26	5 13
22	Thur		4 35	7 25	0 58	27	6 7
23	Frid		4 35	7 25	1 26	28	6 57
24	Satu		4 35	7 25	2 4	29	7 47
25	Sund	2Sund. paft Trini.	4 35	7 25	Sets	30	8 37
26	Mon		4 35	7 25	8 24	1	9 31
27	Tuef		4 35	7 25	9 1	2	10 25
28	Wed	{ Bat.Sulli.Ifl. 76.	4 35	7 25	9 34	3	11 15
29	Thur	} Bat. Monm. 78.	4 36	7 24	10 0	4	Aft. 5
30	Frid		4 36	7 24	10 23	5	0 50

JULY begins on SATURDAY, hath XXXI Days.

Firſt Quarter the 3d day, 5 in the Morning.
Full Moon the 11th day, 6 in the Morning.
Laſt Quarter the 18th day, 8 in the Morning.
New Moon the 25th day, 4 in the Morning.

D. M.	W. days	Feſtivals, Remarkable Days, &c.	Sun rifes H M	Sun ſets. H M	Moon ſets. H. M.	☽ age	High Water H. M.
1	Satu		4 36	7 24	10 47	6	1 45
2	Sund	3 Sund. paſt Trini.	4 36	7 24	11 6	7	2 36
3	Mon		4 37	7 23	11 30	8	3 26
4	Tueſ	Independen. 1776.	4 37	7 23	11 56	9	4 15
5	Wed	Ticon. aband. 77	4 37	7 23	Morn.	10	5 5
6	Thur	Bat.Great Spri.81.	4 38	7 22	0 26	11	5 52
7	Frid		4 38	7 22	0 58	12	6 36
8	Satu	Canon. Gw. Iſl. 76	4 39	7 21	1 36	13	7 21
9	Sund	4 Sund. paſt Trini.	4 39	7 21	2 30	14	8 6
10	Mon		4 40	7 20	3 14	15	8 51
11	Tueſ	Days decreaſe 10m.	4 40	7 20	Rifes	16	9 37
12	Wed		4 41	7 19	8 21	17	10 21
13	Thur		4 42	7 18	9 0	18	11 10
14	Frid		4 42	7 18	9 17	19	Morn.
15	Satu		4 43	7 17	9 39	20	0 3
16	Sund	{ 5 Sund. p. Trin.	4 43	7 17	10 6	21	0 56
17	Mon	} Ston.Pt. tak. 79.	4 44	7 16	10 32	22	1 49
18	Tueſ		4 45	7 15	11 4	23	2 47
19	Wed		4 45	7 15	11 33	24	3 35
20	Thur	Days 14h. 35m.	4 46	7 14	Morn	25	4 28
21	Frid		4 47	7 13	0 23	26	5 23
22	Satu		4 48	7 12	1 28	27	6 18
23	Sund	6 Sund. paſt Trini.	4 49	7 11	2 30	28	7 9
24	Mon		4 50	7 10	3 38	29	8 0
25	Tueſ	Dog Days begin.	4 50	7 10	Sets.	1	8 50
26	Wed		4 51	7 9	7 58	2	9 44
27	Thur		4 52	7 8	8 23	3	10 38
28	Frid	Days 14h. 10m.	4 53	7 7	8 44	4	11 28
29	Satu		4 54	7 6	9 8	5	Aft. 18
30	Sund	7 Sund. paſt Trini.	4 55	7 5	9 30	6	1 4
31	Mon		4 56	7 4	9 54	7	1 50

AUGUST begins on TUESDAY, hath XXXI Days

First Quarter, the 1ft day, 10 in the Afternoon.
Full Moon, the 9th day, 5 in the Afternoon.
Laft Quarter, the 16th day, at Noon.
New Moon, the 23d day, 3 in the Afternoon.
Firft Quarter, the 31ft day, 4 in the Afternoon.

D. M.	W. days	Feftivals, Remarkable Days &c.	Sun rifes H. M	Sun fets H.M	Moon fets H. M.	M. age	High Water H. M.	
1	Tuef	Lammas Day.	4 57	7 3	10 22	8	2	32
2	Wed		4 58	7 2	10 53	9	3	20
3	Thur		4 58	7 2	11 31	10	4	9
4	Frid	Days 14th.	4 59	7 1	morn.	11	4	54
5	Sat.		5 0	6 0	0 16	12	5	41
6	Sun.	8 Sun. p. Tri. &	5 1	6 59	1 8	13	6	29
7	Mon	Transfigurat.	5 2	6 58	2 8	14	7	9
8	Tuef		5 3	6 57	3 9	15	8	56
9	Wed		5 4	6 56	rifes.	16	19	55
10	Thur		5 5	6 55	7 18	17	10	34
11	Frid	Savan. evac. 82.	5 6	6 54	7 39	18	11	23
12	Sat.		5 8	6 52	8 10	19	morn.	
13	Sun.	9 Sund. p. Trin.	5 9	6 51	8 36	20	0	16
14	Mon		5 10	6 50	9 8	21	1	9
15	Tuef		5 11	6 49	9 43	22	2	6
16	Wed	Bat. Camd. 80.	5 13	6 47	10 28	23	3	1
17	Thur		5 14	6 46	11 18	24	3	54
18	Frid.	Days, 13h. 30m.	5 15	6 45	morn.	25	4	48
19	Sat.		5 16	6 44	0 18	26	5	40
20	Sun.	10 Sund. p. Tri.	5 17	6 43	1 24	27	5	36
21	Mon		5 18	6 42	2 32	28	6	30
22	Tuef		5 20	6 40	3 40	29	7	20
23	Wed		5 21	6 39	fets.	30	8	10
24	Thur	St. Bartholom.	5 22	6 38	6 53	1	9	1
25	Frid	Days 13h. 8m.	5 24	6 36	7 15	2	9	54
26	Sat.		5 25	6 35	7 38	3	10	41
27	Sun.	11 Sun. p. Tri. &	5 26	6 34	8 2	4	11	26
28	Mon	B. L. Ifland 76	5 27	6 33	8 28	5	Aft.	12
29	Tuef	St. John Baptift.	5 28	6 32	8 56	6	0	58
30	Wed		5 30	6 30	9 30	7	1	44
31	Thur		5 31	6 29	10 14	8	2	30

SEPTEMBER begins on FRIDAY, hath XXX days.

Full Moon the 8th day, 2 in the Morning.
Last Quarter the 14th day, 6 in the Afternoon.
New Moon the 22d day, 6 in the Morning.
First Quarter the 30th day, 10 in the Morning.

M.W. days	Festivals, Remarkable Days, &c.	Sun rises H M	Sun sets H M	Moon sets H. M.	Age	High Water H. M.
1 Frid		5 32	6 28	10 53	9	3 16
2 Satu		5 33	6 27	11 58	10	4 3
3 Sund	12 Sund. paft Tri.	5 34	6 26	Morn.	11	4 52
4 Mon	Dog-days end.	5 35	6 25	1 8	12	5 41
5 Tuef	Bat. off Chef. 81.	5 36	6 24	2 10	13	6 30
6 Wed		5 38	6 22	3 14	14	7 23
7 Thur	Days 12h. 42m.	5 39	6 21	4 18	15	8 16
8 Frid	Bat. Eutaw. 81.	5 40	6 20	Rifes.	16	9 9
9 Satu		5 41	6 19	6 48	17	10 7
10 Sund	13 Sund. p, Trin.	5 43	6 17	7 15	18	11 3
11 Mon	B. Brandyw. 77.	5 44	6 16	7 48	19	11 59
12 Tuef		5 46	6 14	8 31	20	Morn.
13 Wed	N. Lon. bur. 81.	5 47	6 13	9 26	21	0 56
14 Thur		5 49	6 11	10 26	22	1 49
15 Frid	N. York tak. 76.	5 50	6 10	11 30	23	2 43
16 Satu		5 51	6 9	Morn.	24	3 38
17 Sund	14 Sund. p. Trin.	5 53	6 7	0 38	25	4 31
18 Mon		5 54	6 6	1 48	26	5 21
19 Tuef		5 56	6 4	2 58	27	6 12
20 Wed		5 57	6 3	4 8	28	7 1
21 Thur	St. Matthew.	5 58	6 2	5 2	29	7 51
22 Frid	Day & Night equ.	6 0	6 0	Sets.	1	8 51
23 Satu		6 1	5 59	6 16	2	9 41
24 Sund	15 Sund. p. Trin.	6 3	5 57	6 38	3	10 31
25 Mon	Arnold's plot, 80.	6 4	5 56	7 8	4	11 17
26 Tuef	Phil. taken, 78.	6 5	5 55	7 40	5	Aft. 4
27 Wed		6 7	5 53	8 20	6	0 48
28 Thur		6 8	5 52	9 8	7	1 35
29 Frid	St. Michael.	6 9	5 51	10 8	8	2 21
30 Satu		6 11	5 49	11 8	9	3 7

2

OCTOBER begins on SUNDAY, hath XXXI days.

Full Moon the 7th day, at Noon.
Laſt Quarter the 14th day, 3 in the Morning.
New Moon the 21ſt day, 10 in the Afternoon.
Firſt Quarter the 30th day, 2 in the Morning.

D. M.	W. days	Feſtivals, Remarkable Days, &c.	Sun riſes H M	Sun ſets. HM	Moon riſes. H. M.	M. age	High Water H. M.
1	Sund	16 Sund. paſt Tri.	6 12	5 48	*morn.*	10	3 56
2	Mon	Billing. evacu. 77.	6 13	5 47	0 8	11	4 47
3	Tueſ		6 14	5 46	1 14	12	5 37
4	Wed	Battle German. 77	6 15	5 45	2 30	13	6 28
5	Thur		6 16	5 44	3 38	14	7 17
6	Frid		6 18	5 42	4 42	15	8 10
7	Satu	Bat. Stillwater. 77	6 19	5 41	*Riſes.*	16	9 8
8	Sund	17 Sund. p, Tri. &	6 20	5 40	5 58	17	10 2
9	Mon	Treaty w.Hol.82	6 21	5 39	6 36	18	10 58
10	Tueſ		6 22	5 38	7 28	19	11 55
11	Wed		6 23	5 37	8 26	20	*morn.*
12	Thur	Days 11h. 12m.	6 24	5 36	9 30	21	0 40
13	Frid		6 25	5 35	10 38	22	1 21
14	Satu		6 26	5 34	11 48	23	2 40
15	Sund	Euſopus burnt 77.	6 27	5 33	*morn.*	24	3 34
16	Mon	Burgoyne taken 77	6 29	5 31	0 58	25	4 21
17	Tueſ		6 30	5 30	2 8	26	5 14
18	Wed	Falmouth burnt 75	6 31	5 29	3 8	27	6 4
19	Thur	Cornwallis tak. 81	6 33	5 27	4 8	28	6 54
20	Frid	Bat. Redbank, 77.	6 34	5 26	5 8	29	7 44
21	Satu		6 36	5 24	*ſets.*	30	8 32
22	Sund	19 Sund. paſt Trri.	6 37	5 23	5 21	1	9 16
23	Mon		6 38	5 22	5 48	2	10 2
24	Tueſ		6 40	5 20	6 26	3	10 48
25	Wed	Days 10h. 38m.	6 41	5 19	7 8	4	11 35
26	Thur		6 42	5 18	8 0	5	Aft. 1
27	Frid		6 43	5 17	8 58	6	1 56
28	Satu	Bat. Whitepl. 76.	6 45	5 15	9 59	7	2 46
29	Sund	20 Sund.paſt Trin.	6 46	5 14	11 4	8	3 36
30	Mon		6 47	5 13	*morn.*	9	4 26
31	Tueſ		6 49	5 11	0 8	10	5 17

NOVEMBER begins on WEDNES. hath XXX days.

Full Moon, the 5th day, 10 in the Afternoon.
Last Quarter, the 12th day, 3 in the Afternoon.
New Moon, the 20th day, 5 in the Afternoon.
First Quarter, the 28th day, 4 in the Afternoon.

D.M	W. days	Festivals, Remarkable Days, &c.	Sun rises H. M	Sun sets H M	Moon sets H. M	M age	High Water H. M.
1	Wed	All Saints.	6 50	5 10	1 19	11	6 11
2	Thur		6 51	5 9	2 30	12	7 4
3	Frid	St. John's tak. 75.	6 52	5 8	3 40	13	7 56
4	Satu		6 53	5 7	4 50	14	8 51
5	Sund	21 Sund. p. Trini.	6 54	5 6	rifes.	15	9 44
6	Mon		6 55	5 5	5 18	16	10 43
7	Tuef		6 56	5 4	6 18	17	11 30
8	Wed	Days 10 h. 8m.	6 57	5 3	7 20	18	morn.
9	Thur		6 58	5 2	8 26	19	0 27
10	Frid		7 0	4 0	9 28	20	1 21
11	Satu		7 1	4 59	10 40	21	2 13
12	Sund	22 Sund. p. Trini.	7 2	4 58	11 53	22	3 2
13	Mon	Montreal ta. 75.	7 3	4 57	Morn.	23	3 51
14	Tuef		7 4	4 56	1 0	24	4 41
15	Wed	Fort Miff. ev. 77	7 5	4 55	2 0	25	5 31
16	Thur	Fort Wafh. t. 76	7 6	4 54	3 0	26	6 20
17	Frid		7 8	4 52	4 0	27	7 1
18	Satu	Fort Lee tak. 76	7 9	4 51	5 0	28	7 47
19	Sund	23 Sund. p. Trin.	7 10	4 50	6 0	29	8 33
20	Mon		7 11	4 49	fets.	1	9 19
21	Tuef		7 12	4 48	5 8	2	10 5
22	Wed		7 13	4 47	5 58	3	10 50
23	Thur	Days 9h. 36m.	7 13	4 47	6 49	4	11 37
24	Frid		7 14	4 46	7 50	5	A. 27
25	Satu		7 15	4 45	8 57	6	1 17
26	Sund	24 Sund. p. Trin.	7 16	4 44	10 2	7	2 7
27	Mon		7 16	4 44	11 8	8	2 56
28	Tuef		7 17	44 3	morn.	9	3 47
29	Wed		7 18	4 42	0 11	10	4 44
30	Thur	Provi. Treat. 82	7 18	4 42	1 18	11	5 35

DECEMBER begins on FRIDAY, hath XXXI Days

Full Moon the 5th day, 8 in the Morning.
Laſt Quarter the 12th day, 7 in the Morning
New Moon the 20th day, at Midnight.
Firſt Quarter the 28th day, 3 in the Morning.

D. M.	W. days	Feſtivals, Remarkable Days, &c.	Sun. riſes H M	Sun ſets H M	Moon ſets. H. M.	M. age	High Water H. M.
1	Frid	Days 9h. 22m.	7 19	4 41	2 28	12	0 2
2	Satu		7 20	4 40	3 38	13	7 18
3	Sund	Advent Sunday.	7 20	4 40	4 50	14	8 10
4	Mon		7 21	4 39	6 8	15	8 59
5	Tueſ		7 21	4 39	Riſes	16	9 52
6	Wéd		7 22	4 38	5 54	17	10 40
7	Thur	Bat. Newport, 76.	7 22	4 38	7 8	18	11 35
8	Frid	Bat.G. Bridge 75.	7 23	4 37	8 20	19	Morn.
9	Satu		7 23	4 37	9 35	20	0 27
10	Sund	2 Sund. in Advent.	7 24	4 36	10 38	21	1 19
11	Mon		7 24	4 36	11 42	22	2 12
12	Tueſ		7 24	4 36	Morn.	23	2 52
13	Wed	Days 9h. 12m.	7 24	4 36	0 48	24	3 41
14	Thur	Jerſey overrun, 76.	7 25	4 35	1 54	25	4 31
15	Frid		7 25	4 35	2 49	26	5 17
16	Satu		7 25	4 35	3 46	27	6 4
17	Sund	3 Sund in Advent.	7 25	4 35	4 44	28	6 49
18	Mon		7 25	4 35	5 40	29	7 37
19	Tueſ		7 25	4 35	6 38	1	8 23
20	Wed	Shortest Day.	7 25	4 35	Sets.	2	9 7
21	Thur	St. Thomas.	7 25	4 35	5 28	3	9 55
22	Frid		7 25	4 35	6 33	4	10 46
23	Satu		7 25	4 35	7 38	5	11 35
24	Sund	4 Sund. in Advent.	7 25	4 35	8 46	6	Aft. 24
25	Mon	Chriſtmaſs.	7 25	4 35	9 50	7	1 12
26	Tueſ	Heſſians taken, 76.	7 25	4 35	10 54	8	2 2
27	Wed	St. John the Evan.	7 25	4 35	Morn.	9	2 53
28	Thur	Innocents.	7 25	4 35	0 4	10	3 46
29	Frid	"	7 24	4 36	1 16	11	4 37
30	Satu		7 24	4 36	2 26	12	5 29
31	Sund	Montgom. fell, 75.	7 24	4 36	3 38	13	6 26

E C L I P S E S.

THERE will be five Eclipses this year, three of the Sun and two of the Moon.

The 1ft is of the Moon, January 14th, the former part vifible, and the latter invifible.

Beginning, 14th Day, at	6h.	38m.	}	Morning.
Middle, - - -	7	49		
End, - - -	9	0		
Duration, - -	2	22		

Digits eclipsed near 5, on the Moon's fouth limb.

N. B. This eclipfe begins but 38 minutes before the fun rifes ; fo only the beginning is vifible.

The 2d is of the fun, January 29th, at 40 minutes paft 6 o'clock in the evening, invifible.

The 3d is of the Moon, July 11th, vifible in part, and calculated as follows :

Beginning of vifibility,	4h.	1m.	} Morning.
Beginning of total darknefs,	5	29	
Middle, - -	5	55	
End of total darknefs,	6	7	
End of the Eclipfe,	7	30	

Digits Eclipfed near 13

N. B. This eclipfe begins but 31 minutes before the Sun rifes ; fo only the beginning is vifible.

The 4th is of the Sun, July 25th, at 53 minutes paft 3 o'clock in the morning, invifible.

The 5th is of the Sun, December 20th, at 52 minutes paft 11 o'clock in the morning, invifible.

Moon's Latitude, 1° 22' South.

Common Notes and Moveable Feasts, for 1786.

Golden Number	1	Shrove Sunday, Feb. 26.
Epact	0	Eafter Sunday, April 16.
Dominical Letter	A	Afcention Day, May 25.
Cycle of the Sun	3	Whitfunday, June 4.

2*   B 2

TABLE of DOLLARS, &c.

Number of Dollars.	New-York and N. Carolina			N. Hampſh. Maſſachu. Rhd. Iſland, Connecticut & Virginia.			N.-Jersey, Pennſylvan. Maryland, and Delaware.			S. Carolina, and Georgia.		
	£.	s.	d.	£.	s.	d.	£.	s.	d.	£.	s.	d.
1	0	8	0	0	6	0	0	7	6	0	4	8
2	0	16	0	0	12	0	0	15	0	0	9	4
3	1	4	0	0	18	0	1	2	6	0	14	0
4	1	12	0	1	4	0	1	10	0	0	18	8
5	2	0	0	1	10	0	1	17	6	1	3	4
6	2	8	0	1	16	0	2	5	0	1	8	0
7	2	16	0	2	2	0	2	12	6	1	12	8
8	3	4	0	2	8	0	3	0	0	1	17	4
9	3	12	0	2	14	0	3	7	6	2	2	0
10	4	0	0	3	0	0	3	15	0	2	6	8
11	4	8	0	3	6	0	4	2	6	2	11	4
12	4	16	0	3	12	0	4	10	0	2	16	0
13	5	4	0	3	18	0	4	17	6	3	0	8
14	5	12	0	4	4	0	5	5	0	3	5	4
15	6	0	0	4	10	0	5	12	6	3	10	0
16	6	8	0	4	16	0	6	0	0	3	14	8
17	6	16	0	5	2	0	6	7	6	3	19	4
18	7	4	0	5	8	0	6	15	0	4	4	0
19	7	12	0	5	14	0	7	2	6	4	8	8
20	8	0	0	6	0	0	7	10	0	4	13	4
21	8	8	0	6	6	0	7	17	6	4	18	0
22	8	16	0	6	12	0	8	5	0	5	2	8
23	9	4	0	6	18	0	8	12	6	5	7	4
24	9	12	0	7	4	0	9	0	0	5	12	0
25	10	0	0	7	10	0	9	7	6	5	16	8
26	10	8	0	7	16	0	9	15	0	6	1	4
27	10	16	0	8	2	0	10	2	6	6	6	0
28	11	4	0	8	8	0	10	10	0	6	10	8
29	11	12	0	8	14	0	10	17	6	6	15	4
30	12	0	0	9	0	0	11	5	0	7	0	0
35	14	0	0	10	10	0	13	2	6	8	3	4
40	16	0	0	12	0	0	15	0	0	9	6	8
45	18	0	0	13	10	0	16	17	6	10	10	0
50	20	0	0	15	0	0	18	15	0	11	13	4
55	22	0	0	16	10	0	20	12	6	12	16	8
60	24	0	0	18	0	0	22	10	0	14	0	0
70	28	0	0	21	0	0	26	5	0	16	6	8

TABLE of DOLLARS, &c.

Number of Dollars	New-York, and N.Carolina.			N. Hampsh. Massachu. Rhd. Island, Connecticut & Virginia.			N.-Jersey, Pennsylvan. Maryland, and Delaware.			S. Carolina, and Georgia.		
80	32	0	0	24	0	0	£30	0	0	£18	13	4
90	36	0	0	27	0	0	33	15	0	21	0	0
100	40	0	0	30	0	0	37	10	0	23	6	8
200	80	0	0	60	0	0	75	0	0	46	13	4
300	120	0	0	90	0	0	112	10	0	70	0	0
400	160	0	0	120	0	0	150	0	0	93	6	8
500	200	0	0	150	0	0	187	10	0	116	13	4
1000	400	0	0	300	0	0	375	0	0	233	6	8
2000	800	0	0	600	0	0	750	0	0	466	13	4
2500	1000	0	0	750	0	0	937	10	0	583	6	8
3000	1200	0	0	900	0	0	1125	0	0	700	0	0
4000	1600	0	0	1200	0	0	1500	0	0	933	6	8
5000	2000	0	0	1500	0	0	1875	0	0	1166	13	4
6000	2400	0	0	1800	0	0	2250	0	0	1400	0	0
7000	2800	0	0	2100	0	0	2625	0	0	1633	6	8
8000	3200	0	0	2400	0	0	3000	0	0	1866	13	4
9000	3600	0	0	2700	0	0	3375	0	0	2100	0	0
10000	4000	0	0	3000	0	0	3750	0	0	2333	6	8

TABLE of English and French Crowns as they pass in the states of New-York and North-Carolina.

No.	L.	s.	d.	No.	L.	s.	d.	No.	L.	s.	d.
1	0	9	0	15	6	15	0	29	13	1	0
2	0	18	0	16	7	4	0	30	13	10	0
3	1	7	0	17	7	13	0	40	18	0	0
4	1	16	0	18	8	2	0	50	22	10	0
5	2	5	0	19	8	11	0	60	27	0	0
6	2	14	0	20	9	0	0	70	31.10		0
7	3	3	0	21	9	9	0	80	36	0	0
8	3	12	0	22	9	18	0	90	40	10	0
9	4	1	0	23	10	7	0	100	45	0	0
10	4	10	0	24	10	16	0	200	90	0	0
11	4	19	0	25	11	5	0	300	135	0	0
12	5	8	0	26	11	14	0	400	180	0	0
13	5	17	0	27	12	3	0	500	225	0	0
14	6	6	0	28	12	12	0	1000	450	0	0

A TABLE to afcertain the value of fundry Coins of Gold, as regulated by the Chamber of Commerce; which fhews, at one view, their value in Great Britain.——*N. B. There has been a late regulation made by the Affembly of South Carolina, that English Guineas must weigh 5 dwt. 7 grs. Piftoles 4 dwt. 6 grs. and Moidores 6 dwt. 16 grs.*

SPECIES.	Standard Weight.		New-York Curr.			Sterling Mon. of G. Brita.		
	dwt.	gr,	L.	s.	d.	L.	s.	d.
Double Johannes -	18	0	6	8	0	3	12	0
Single ditto -	9	0	3	4	0	1	16	0
Half ditto -	4	12	1	12	0	0	18	0
Quarter ditto -	2	6	0	16	0	0	9	0
Caroline ditto -	6	8	1	18	0	1	2	0
Spanish Doubloons	17	0	6	0	0	3	6	0
Two piftole -	8	12	3	0	0	1	12	0
One ditto -	4	6	1	10	0	0	16	0
Englifh Guinea -	5	6	1	17	4	1	1	0
Half ditto -	2	15	0	18	8	0	10	6
French Guinea -	5	4	1	16	4	1	1	0
Half ditto -	2	14	0	18	2	0	10	6
Chequin -	2	4	0	14	6	0	8	0
Moidore -	6	18	2	8	0	1	7	0

TABLE of HALF-JOHANNES.

No.	L.	s.	No.	L.	s.	No.	L.	s.	No.	L.	s.
1	3	4	14	44	16	27	86	8	300	960	0
2	6	8	15	48	0	28	89	12	400	1280	0
3	9	12	16	51	4	29	92	16	500	1600	0
4	12	16	17	54	8	30	96	0	600	1920	0
5	16	0	18	57	12	35	112	0	700	2240	0
6	19	4	19	60	16	40	128	0	800	2560	0
7	22	8	20	64	0	45	144	0	900	2880	0
8	25	12	21	67	4	50	160	0	1000	3200	0
9	28	16	22	70	8	60	192	0	2000	6200	0
10	32	0	23	73	12	70	224	0	3000	9600	0
11	35	4	24	76	16	80	256	0	4000	12800	0
12	38	8	25	80	0	90	288	0	5000	16000	0
13	41	12	26	83	4	100	320	0	10000	32000	0
						200	640	0			

TABLE of GUINEAS,

Reduced into New-York Currency.

Guins	L.	s.	d.	Guins.	L.	s.	d.
1	1	17	4	31	57	17	4
2	3	14	8	32	59	14	8
3	5	12	0	33	61	12	0
4	7	9	4	34	63	9	4
5	9	6	8	35	65	6	8
6	11	4	0	36	67	4	0
7	13	1	4	37	69	1	4
8	14	18	8	38	70	18	8
9	16	16	0	39	72	16	0
10	18	13	4	40	74	13	4
11	20	10	8	41	76	10	8
12	22	8	0	42	78	8	0
13	24	5	4	43	80	5	4
14	26	2	8	44	82	2	8
15	28	0	0	45	84	0	0
16	29	17	4	46	85	17	4
17	31	14	8	47	87	14	8
18	33	12	0	48	89	12	0
19	35	9	4	49	91	9	4
20	37	6	8	50	93	6	8
21	39	4	0	60	112	0	0
22	41	1	4	70	130	13	4
23	42	18	8	80	149	6	8
24	44	16	0	90	168	0	0
25	46	13	4	100	186	13	4
26	48	10	8	200	373	6	8
27	50	8	0	300	560	0	0
28	52	5	4	400	746	13	4
29	54	2	8	500	933	6	8
30	56	0	0	1000	1866	13	4

THE

New-York Directory.

A

ARDEN John, board-merchant, Number 106, Queen-Street
Ash Tho. Winds. chair maker, 31, John-st
Atkinson Francis. merchant, 223, Q.street
Allingham Charles, and company, merchants, 196, Queen-street
Abremse A. shopkeeper, 42, Water-street
Abbot & Kanberry, tailors, 44, Water-st.
Asbridge R. conveyaucer, 27, Smith-street
Asten J. shoemaker, 31, Nassau-street
Anderson A. joiner, 17, Maiden-lane
Anderson Elb. shopkeeper, 5, Maiden-l.
Anderson J. shopkeeper, 89, Water-street
Acklay A. iron-monger, 7, Broad-street
Attwood T. Bridgen, doctor, 11, Dock-st.

Arding Charles, doctor, 13, corner William and Beekman streets

Afflock Robert, merchant, 60, Wm. street

Antwerp Van & M'Ewen, grocers, 3, Flym.

Aicken And. shopkeeper, 40, Broadway

Anderson James, shoemaker, 65, Broadway

Arthur John, merchant, 160, Queen-street

Aorson Aaron, 28, Nassau-street

Ashfield John, baker, 44, William-street

B

Barham Mrs. tavern-keeper, 18, Broadway

Betts John, distiller, 3, Whitehall

Byrn William, Esq. 36, George-street

Bickers John, carpenter, 32, Geo. street

Brewer Peter, grocer, 124, Queen-street

Brevoort John, merchant, 161, Q. street

Berrien Peter, 103, Queen-street

Bawie Ann, shopkeeper, 60, Broad-way

Bayly William, merchant, 58, Broadway

Bache Abraham, rev. of the church of England, 29, Smith-street

Besley and Goodwin, druggists and apothecaries, 229, Queen-street

Bassett Francis, pewterer, 218, Q. street

Burger John, goldsmith, 207, Queen-street

Bredhurst Samuel, physician and apothecary, 64, Queen-street

Bowne Geo. merchant, 37, Queen-street

Brevoort Abr. merchant, 26, Queen-street

Bradford & M'Ewen, plumb. 147, Wat.st
Burke G. grocer, 161, Water-street
Backhouse, merchant, 163, Water-street
Beeking Wm. grocer, 33, Han. square.
Berry & Rogers, 35, merchants, Han. squ.
Bourghell J. watch maker, 192, Water-st.
B. & Browne, shopkeepers, 14, Wm. street
Buckle William, merchant, 9, Water-street
Banks John, tailor, 12, Water-street
Bleecker J. and L. brokers, 20, Water-st.
Bard John, merchant, 46, Water-street
Byvanck John, merchant, 56, Water-street
Biggs Thomas, instrument-maker, 60, facing Beekman's-slip
Byarr Samuel, grocer, 75, Broadway
Brooks M. painter & glazier, 51, Crown-st.
Bewie Daniel, grocer, 38, Crown-street
Bostwick And. merchant, 37, Smith-street
Bryant William, Mr. 1, Smith-street
Bramble James, whitesmith, 49, King-street
Bard Samuel, doctor, 46, Broad-street
Barrow T. merchant, 58, Broad-street
Beckman J. Jas. merchant, 20, Maiden-l.
Bend Grove, shopkeeper, 16, Smith-street
Broome J. merchant, 6, Hanover-square
Barclay Jas. merchant, 14, Hanover-square
Blackwell Joseph, merchant, 21, Han. squ.
Buclin T. and W. earthen-ware and glass
    merchants, 69, Water-street
Bleecker L. Anth. 40, auctioneer, Wall-st.

Brower N. merchant, 95, Water-street
Bancker Evert, merchant, 5, Wall-street
Burres Lawrence, grocer, 64, Wall-street
Blagge Benj. esq. alderman, 63, Cherry-st.
Barker B. w.& clock-maker, 57, Cherry-st.
Bleecker R. inn-keeper, 57, Cherry-street
Beckman Theoph. merchant, 9, Cherry-st.
Burnside James, Mr. 67, Cherry-street
Bowne Daniel, merchant, 6, Cherry-street
Burras Benj. shoemaker, 3, Broad-street
Brower J. upholsterer, 28, Broad-street
Brinckerhooff Abr. merchant 10, Dock-st.
Blair Archd. stock-broker, 16, L. Dock-st.
Bruce P. & R. merchants, 3, Front-street
Brand Henry, tobacconist, 6, Beekman-st.
Bond Abraham, grocer, 6, Whitehall
Boyd James, grocer, 2, Pearl-street
Brasher E. goldsmith, 1 Cherry-street
Burns John, merchant, 2, Flymarket
Baldwin, B. grocer, 19, Flymarket
Bussing N. tailor, Little Queen-street
Brown Tho. stone-cutter, Thame-street
Bausell John, grocer, Partition-street
Buskirk S. tin-man, 39, Broadway
Bayly William, tin-man, 59, Broadway
Bauman S. grocer, 62, Broadway
Buchanan & Thomp. merchants, 243, Q.st.
Browne J. surgeon& dentist, 9, L.Q.street
Beekman & Sons, merchants,241, Q.street
Burtsell Wm. shoemaker, 12, L. Dock-st.

3

Beekman Van Beuen, 80, William-street
O'Bryans Captain, 11, Brownjohn's wharf
Byrne,Dorsten&Colburn,merchants,Flym.
Bay A. S. goldsmith, 66, Smith-street

C.

Colles B. John, merchant, 12, Dock-street
Coster, Brothers and co. 20, Dock-street
Childs Francis, printer, 189, Water-street
Currie Jo. confectioner, 52, Smith-street
Cuthbert Sam. mast-maker 18, L.Q.street
Clarkson David, merchant, 73, King-street
Constable, Rucker, and company, mer-
    chants, Dock-street
Cortlandt G. and company, ironmongers
    42, Dock-street
Cape John, city tavern, , Broadway
Costigin Johnson, tav.keeper, LowerBatt.
Cowen Solomon, 4, Whitehall
Cheesman ——, tavern-keeper, Broadway
Campbell Thomas, potter, 29, Geo. street
Cogswell James Mason 219, surgeon and
    apothecary, Queen-street
Crabb Tho. merchant, 212, Queen-street
Crosbey Dr. 59, Queen-street
Comfort & Joshua Sands, merchants, 50,
    Queen-street
Campbell John, 31, Hanover-square
Craige, Wanright and company, apothe-
    caries, 27, Wall-street

Campbell Saml. bookseller, 41, Han. squ.

Cox Isaac, merchant, 194, Queen-street

Cocks Robert, merchant, 4, Wm. street

Chandler Metleck, shopkeeper, 11, Wm.st.

Crone David, tailor, 7, between Fly-market and Murray's-wharf

Curson Samuel, merchant, 208, Water-st.

Coon G. grocer, 31, Fly-market

Cuyler Mrs. boarding and lodging-house for gentlemen, 45, Fly-market

Carter A. shoemaker, Cherry-street

Cock A. school-mistress, 9, Crown-street

Carmer Nich. cabinet-maker, 34, Maid.la.

Charlton John, doctor, 37, Broad-street

Cautant David, windsor-c. m. 57, Broad-st.

Ceary James, lodging-house, 66, Broadway

Carr M. Mrs. milliner, 8, Maiden-lane

Christie James, earthen-ware and glass merchant, 12, Maiden-lane

Campbell D. esq; merchant, 18, Smith-st.

Clarkson D. and co. 13, Hanover-square

Cocks E. merchant, 75, Water-street

Clopper Corn. merchant, 67 Water-street

Caffing Francis, porter house, 26. Wall-st.

Crygier, punch & p. house, 69, Cherry-st.

Cruger Nicholas, merchant, 16, Duke-st.

Colinac John, merchant, 48, Dock-street

Clark Wm. innkeeper, 2, L. Water-street

Cock Asher, tavernkeeper, Crane-wharf

Chace John, tailor, 18, Broadway

C

Coll V. John, tailor, 48, Cherry-street
Clark Thomas, lumber-yard,Cherry-street
Clement John, grocer, 17, Flymarket
Cornell Gilbert, snuff mercht. 12, Flymar.
Cock Henry, merchant, Cortlandt-street
Cochran John, doctor, 96, Broadway
Cortlandt V. J. sugar-baker, 17, Broadway
Cox Albian, merchant, 240, Queen-street
Cromie Francis, shopkeeper, 62, Wm.-st.
Cockle Fred. ironmonger, &c. 193, Q. st.
Corre J. hotel, 52, Smith-street
Campbell S. merchant, 4, Hanover-square
Cockcroft Wm. merchant, 39, Water-st.
Colles Christopher, fig-blue manufacturer,
&c. 2, Lower-battery
Constable, Rucker, and company, mer-
chants, Mill-street
Cooper Ananias, doctor, 47, Dock-street
Coffee M. P. teacher of languages, 21,
Nassau-street
Cockran John, carpenter, 31, Duke-street
Cocks J. merchant, 83, Water-street
Connelly ——, tavernkeeper, 27, Geo. st.
Coenrad W. Ham baker, 19, Broad-st.

D

Dramer Peter, merchant, 2, Whitehall
Daly Mrs. shopkeeper, , Broadway
Dorman Mrs. 126, Queen-street ·
Douglass Nathan, school-master, 127, Q.st.

Delaplein N. & W. merchants, 211, Q. st.
Donovan Tim. tobacconist, 57, Q. street
Donaldson J. shoemaker, 76 Q. street
Dodds T. organ and musical instrument
   maker, 76 Q. street
Duleey & company, merchants, 51, Q. st.
Desbrosees James, 9, Q. street
Desbrosees Mrs. 8, Q. street
Dudley Wm. board. & lodg. 151, Wat. st.
Douglas Benj. tailor, 27, Smith-street
Dewhurst John, merchant, 90. Water-st.
Duychinck G. medicine store, 13, Wat. st.
Dixon J. merchant, 94, Wm.-street
Daft Tho. watchmaker 33, Maiden-lane
Debaw Mary Mrs. earthen-ware, Maiden-l.
Dibiny Mrs. 18, Wall-street
Deril Wm. earthen-ware. 79, Water-street
Denning Wm. Esq. 10 Wall-street
Dominick Fran. lumber-yard, 7, Cherry-st.
Dalton John, surgeon, 67 Broad-street.
Duine John, 8, Broad-street
Duncin and Ferguson, 10, Flymarket,
Deane Richard, distiller, lower end of
   Greenwich-street.
Dash B. John, tin, copper and ironmon-
   gry store, 67, Broadway
Durning Richd. merchant, 202, Q. street
Douglass Geo. grocer, 14, Flymarket
Delafield John, broker, &c. 28, Water-st.

Dewint John, merchant, 12, Duke-street,
Delap Samuel, 239, Queen-street
Depeyster W. A.
Draper Geo. doctor, &c. 47, Han.-square
Degro Peter, painter and glazier, 136,Q.st.
Deleplane Jo. Quaker sperker, 132, Q. st.
Dale Samuel, 78, Queen-street,
Deremur Nicholas, hatter,85,Queen-street
Douglass Geo. & S. merchants, 233, Q. st.
Dobson Tho. merchant, 330, Q. street

E

Egbert Moses, , Whitehall
Eckert Catharine, gent. 22, George street
Earl A. Mrs. shopkeeper, , Broadway
Eustace Edward, shoemak. 122, Broadway
Ellis John, merchant, 25, Broadway
Ellsworth John, hatter, 23, Broadway
Ellison Wm. joiner, 20, King-street
Elsworth V. merchant, 19, Maiden-lane
Edgar Wm. esq. 7, Wall-street
Egbert James, carman, 2, Dock-street
Eccles Wm. merchant, 10, Hunter's Quay

F

Franks D. conveyancer, &c. 66, Broadw.
Forbes A. Wm. saddler, 78, Broadway
Farfor Alex. school-master, , Whitehall
Fredenburgh Isaac, shoemak. , Broadw.
Faish Michael, mason 112, Queen-street

Forbes A. Wm. carpenter, 98, Q. street
Franklin Thomas, merchant, 94, Q. street
Fisher Leonard, surg. barber, 116,Q.street
Fraiser Wm. ship-carpenter, 79, Q. street
Franklin Samuel, merchant 183, Q. street
Flight Joseph merchant, 28, Queen-street
Foster John, merchant, 133, Water-street
Fred. and Philip Rhinelander, merchants,
   168, Water-street
Fat & la Forgue, furriers, 23,Water-street
Fleming John, auctioneer, 54, Smith-street
Fortune John, grocer, 8, Garden-street
Forbes G. Wm. goldsmith, 88, Broadway.
Fallum Michael, grocer, 1, Nassau-street
Fox G. tailor, 6, Smith-street
Fisher John Mr. 20, Duke-street
Fleming Mrs. mantua-maker, 22, Duke-st.
Forest & Cleminson, grocers, 2 L.Water-st.
Francis John, board. & lodg. 3, Dock-st.
Freeman John Captain, 30, Cherry-street
Franklin John, merchant, 35,Cherry-street
Fine Jacob, merchant, 9, Flymarket
Forbes P. Mrs. shopkeeper,73, Broadway
Foxcroft John,   91, Broadway
Fueter Daniel, goldsmith, 94, Broadway
Fell & Graham, merchts. 2, Cruger's-wh.
Franklin Tho. jun. auctioneer, 14,H.squa
Ferris Jonathan farmer, Frogsneck, West
   Chester

G

Goodberlat John, tailor, , Broadway
Gilbert Wm. silversmith, , Broadway
Garness Nelly, tailor. 116, Queen-street
Gesner John, grocer, 50, Chatham-street
Green Richard, painter, gilder, glazier, &
  colourman, 237, Queen-street
Getfield Benj. breeches & leather dresser,
  20, Queen-street
Gaine Hugh, bookseller,&c. 36,Han.squ.
Gault Robert, merchant, 30, Han. square
Gaine R. John, bookseller, 44, Han. squ.
Grandine John, shoemaker, 1, Wm. street
Gourlay, Mrs. milliner, 13, Wm. street
Gillespie Jas.& Tho. merchts. 15, Wm. st.
Gardiner Thomas, merchant, 85, Wm. st.
Grier, Brooks & co. merchts. 88, Wm. st.
Grimes, school-master, 7, King-street
Gano John, minister of the baptist church,
  14, King-street
Gillelan John, grocer, 9, Garden-street
Gardiner Noah, shoemaker, 32, Maiden-l.
Graham John, tin-plate-worker, 11, M. l.
Garbrane Peter, turner & umbrella-ma-
  ker, 62, Maiden-lane
Governeur Isaac, sen. 14, Smith-street
Gamble A. merchant, 22,Hanover-square
Goold Edward, 48, Wall-street
Gilchrist John doctor, 66, Cherry-street

Goelet John, merchant, 26, Cherry-street
Goodeve John, chandler, 55, Broadway
Goelet John, merchant, 5, Duke-street
Griffiths John, hair-dresser, 18, Chath-row
George J. currier, 57, Dock-street
Green John, grocer, 6, Moore-street
Griswood J. 121, Water-street
Grant James, grocer, 33, Roosevelt-street
Garner D. tailor, 44, Cherry-street
Greswald J. distiller, 19, Cherry-street
Graham James, merchant, 25, Cherry st.
Gib M. A. painter & glazier, 80, Broadw.
Guion Carthy &co. merchts.33, L. Dock-st
Goforth Wm. merchant, 139, Water-st.
Glover John, merchant, 71, Wm. street
Gilford Samuel, merchant, 77, Wm. street
Gomez Moses, 203, Water-street
Goelet Peter, merchant, 48, Han. square

H

Hall, inn-keeper, Harlaem Heights,
Hendricks Carman, 28, George-street
Hobley Abr. tavernkeep. 143, Q. street
Hitchcock John, carman, 117, Q. street
Hegeman Peter, shopkeeper, 131, Q. st.
Hyatt Caleb, innkeeper, 151, Q. street
Hollwel Sam. house carpenter, 105, Q. st.
Hitchcock, D. house carpenter & under-
taker, 89, Queen-street
Hogland John, saddler, &c. 95, Q. street

Henderson Hugh,mercht. 24,Queen-street
Howe General, 156, Water-street
Hewxhurst & Seaman, earthen-ware house
  178, Water-street
Hull Oliver, medicine store 26, Han. squ.
Hunt John, merchant, 36, Han. square
Hendrick Uriah, ironmonger, 43, H. squ.
Harrison Richard, esq. 186,Water-street
Harry Peters, 3, William-street
Hone and Moore merch. 19, Wm. street
Hallett Jacob, grocer, 2, Water-street
Hazard & Brewster, ironmong. 16,Wat.st.
Herring Abrm. merchant, 50, Water-st.
Haviland E. merchant, 65, Water-street
Howe and Prince, merchants, 86, Wat.st.
Hogg E. school-master, 58, Crown-street
Hay Samuel, merchant, 86, Wm. street
Harris C. merchant, 93, Wm. street
Hodge Robert, book-binder, and station-
  er, 38, Maiden-lane
Hill Wm. & co. merchants, 39, Maid. l.
Haron Dens. tailor, 41, Maiden-lane
Hicks Miss   45, Maiden-lane
Haviland and Lawrence, 48, Crown-street
Henry John, Mr. 43, Crown-street
Heymets, tailor, 30, Crown-street
Haughton Thomas, 45, Smith-street
Heyer Walter, tavernkeep. 75, King-st.
House A. baker, 43, Broad-street
Hicks John, doctor, 47, Nassau-street

Halstead B. goldsmith, 13, Maiden-lane
Heb. Mrs. shopkeeper, 10, Maiden-lane
Harding John, shopkeeper 29, Smith-st.
Huck Michael, shopkeeper 1, Han. square
Harsin George, tailor 46, Wall-street
Hamilton and co. distillery, 101, Water-st
Hunt T. merchant, 104, Water-street
Hamilton and Miller, vendue and com-
    mission store, 33, Water-street
Harding S. Captain, 65, Cherry-street
Haight Ben. saddler, 53, Broadway
Haight&VanVoorhies, merchts. 9,Dock-st
Hallet David, tailor, 28, Dock-street
Hopper Andrew, merchant, 71,Chath-row
Hath Thomas, carpenter,   , Chatham-r.
Hanshew Mrs. tutoress, 64,Beekman-street
Hillyer Wm. tavern-keeper 1, L. Wat. st.
Hacker H. merchant, 8, Flymarket
Harman Frederick, doctor, 35, Broadway
Houseman John, painter,&c. 48,Broadway
Houseman William, tailor 70, Broadway
Hoffman Mrs. grocer, 71, Broadway
Haviland, ——, merchant, 164, Queen-st.
Hunter E. merchant, 163, Queen-street
Henry John, merchant, 209, Queen-street
Hart Lion, merchant, 4, Little-Dock-st.
Huck Paul, shoemaker, 39, Wm. street
Hearne, livery-stables, 56, Gold-street
Hoffman Mrs. 27, John-street
Henry John 209, merchant, Queen-street

Hazard Ebenezer, esq. 55, Broadway
Hawxhurst Nathaniel watch-m. 204, Q. st.
Haydock Henry, merchant, 197, Q. street
Haydock & Warr, merchants, 49,Q.street
Hopkins Sam. & co. merchants, 30, Q. st.
Himele Jas. watch-maker, 17.9, Wm. street
Hagermans Jacob, merchant, 72, Wm. st.
Hosack Alex. woolen& linen draper 78, do.
Hamtrack John, 15, Little-Queen-street
Hunt Thomas, 142, Water-street
Hamersley Andrew, ironmonger, and dry
    good merchant, 46, Hanover-square

I

Jones Isaac, coach-maker, , Broadway
Isiah Rogers, W. Clerk 123, Queen-st.
Johnson Ogden, 232, Q. street
Johnson Wm. ironmonger, 171, Water-st.
Johnson Robert, merchant, 177, Water-st.
Jacobs Wm. shoemaker, 180, Water-st.
Isaac Joshua, merchant, 8, Water-street
Jauncey M. doctor, 15, King-street
Johnson David, esq. 17, Wall-street
Isaac A. tailor, 3, Princess-street
Jemmison Neil, merchant. 5, Han. square
Ireland John, merchant, 68, Water-street
Jonas Lyon, furrier 21, Broad-street
Jacobs Benj. merchant, 10, Duke-street
Judah S. Benj. merchant, 22, Dock-street
Jacob E. carpenter, 4, Thames-street

Jay Frederick, auctioneer, 11, Q. street
Jones Herbert Mr. 55, Wm. street
Irwing Wm. merchant, 75, Wm. street
I'ans Francis, merchant, 51, Broad-street
Judson David, 59, Water-street
Intire M. Neal, 19, Peck-slip

K

Kollock Shepard, printer and bookseller,
  corner of Wall and Water streets
Kennedy Henry, innkeeper, 13, Geo. street
Kenner Jonathan, carpenter, 152, Q. street
Kitchel Samuel, cooper, 108, Q. street
Kip James, brass-founder, 59, Broadway
Keating John, merchant, 220, Queen-street
Kemble Wm. watch-maker, 62, Q. street
Keating John, merchant 20, Queen-street
Kelly M. innkeeper 137, Water-street
King John, 2, William-street
King Abram.& John, merchts, 16 Wm.st.
Kip Henry, merchant, 25, King-street
Kip H. Henry, inspector of pot and pearl
  Ashes, 25, King-street
King John, tailor, 56, Broad-street
Kemble Peter, esq. 14, Smith-street
Kipp R. upholsterer, 7, Smith-street
Kirkby Wm. pewterer, 23, Dock-street
Kip Leonard, merchant, 21 Dock-street
Kip Jas. & Henry, merchts. 40, L. Dock-st.
King Francis, innkeeper, 10, Front-street

4

Kunze, Chris. John doctor, 24, Chat. row
Kemper John, painter, 3, Partition-street
Kenyon Wm. painter, 190, Queen-street
King and co. merchants, 65 Wm. street
Kempton Sam. tin-plate, copper and iron
    smith, 197, Water-street
Keating Charles, 15, New-Dock-street
Kip and Duryea, merchants, 45, Han.squa.

L

Lomesny James, 34, George-street
Lawrence J. merchant, 162, Queen-street
Livingston Mrs. 51, Queen-street
Leath Mrs. 107, Queen-street
Labec Catharine, shopkeeper, 82, Q.street
Lecock and Intle, winsr-chairm. 71, Q. st.
Lott and Van Horn, merchants, 214,Q .st.
Lenox Robert, merchant, 210, Q. street
Livingston G. Robt. 1, Queen-street
Lawrence A. merchant, 132, Water-street
Laight Wm. merchant, 136, Water-street
Leary D. tailor, 169, Water-street
Leipper and Gray, merchants 36, H. squ.
Leary Wm. grocer, 182, Water-street
Ludlow C. esq. 184, Water-street
Loudon Sam. printer, &c. 5, Water-street
Lencester B. shipwright, 73, Cherry-street
Lawrence John, doctor, 53, Smith-street
Livingston John, esq. 71, King-street
Lynch and Stoughton, merchants, 9, P.st.

Lee and Ferguson, 24, Nassau-street
Lewis James, tailor, 2, Garden-street
Lynch Dominick, 9, princess-street
Laughern Arthur, merchant, 54, M. lane
Ludlow and Goold, 47, Wall-street
Laehr Christian, tailor, 42, Smith-street
Lawrence Tho. merchant, 61, Cherry-st.
Leary Joseph, chocolate-mak. 15, Broad-st.
Lott Abraham, merchant, 15, Duke-street
Levy Rayman, merchant, 7, Duke-street
Leake G. John, gentleman, 5, Fair-street
Lawrence Richd. china, glass and earthen
    ware merchant, 26, Golden-hill street
Latham J. esq. 13, Cherry-street
Lefferts & Suydem, merchts, 40, Water-st.
Lasher John, grocer, &c. 28, Fly-market.
Lefoy Thomas, hatter, , Broadway
Lasley S. Mrs. shopkeeper, 41, Broadway
Livingston J. clergyman of the Dutch
    church, 79, Broadway
Lawrence & Morris, 83, Broadway, or at
    their store, corner Duke-street&Old-slip
Livingston John, esq. 51, Queen-street
Lamont Æneas, Intelligence-office, and
    broker, 22, Water-street
Lente L. Crist. merchant, 33, Han-square
Ludlam Henry, bathing-house, North-R.
Low Nicholas, merchant, 216, Water st.
Lawrence Eff. merchant, 227, Queen-st.

Longley Thomas, shoemaker, 57, Wm.st.
Lockwood John mercht. 74, Wm. street

M

Monerie Mrs. gent. 35, George street
Merchant Henry, innkeeper, 9, Geo. street
Martling Mrs. tavern-keeper, 4, Geo. st.
Miller John, hair-dresser, , Broadway
Manly Robert, coachmaker, , Broadway
Macabee Mrs. grocer, 142, Queen-street
Mackay Donald, hair-dresser,157,Q.street
Montgomery Mrs. 51, Queen-street
Mead James, merchant, 17, Roosevelt-st.
Montanue Isaac, grocer, 83, Queen-street
Myers J. tavern-keeper, 30, John-street
Moore B. tobacconist, 45, John-street
Mitchel Andrew, merchant, 236, Q.street
More Richard, doctor, 229, Queen-street
Moorewood & co. merchants,222,Q. street
Mitchel H. watch-maker, 201, Q. street.
Montaudevert Jas. merchant, 202, Q. st.
Myers Wm. hair-dresser, 62, Queen-street
Murray John, jun. merchant, 38, Q.street
Muligan H. merchant tailor, 23 Q.street
Miller E. jun. merchant, 14, Queen-street
Merkel Lott, furrier, 6, Queen-street
Muisson James, apothecary, 150, Water-st.
Mahon William, & co. merchants, 159,
    Queen-street
Maule Thomas, merchant, 40, Han.-squ.
Meales Josh. & co. merchts. 191, Wat. st.

Murro & M'Graith, merch. 23,Maid-lane
Mould Walter, 23, William-street
Morgan J. jun. paint. & glaz. 15,Wat.st.
Miller Peter, tobacconist, 19, Water-street
Morton S. M. merchant, 215, Wat.-street
Macgill Robert, bookseller, 212, Wat.-st.
Mitchell & Herbertson, 42, Golden-hill
Mowatt John, iron-monger, 87, Wm.-st.
Meeks Edward, blacksmith, 5, Crown-st.
Moutmye Ab. brass-founder, 13, King-st.
Mercein Andrew, baker, 16, King-street
Montgomery Robert, 19, King-street
Miller Mary Mrs. 55, King-street
Mason John, minister, of the Seceder
    church, 7, Nassau-street.
Mooney Wm. upholsterer, 14, Nassau-st.
Murphy Mary, tavernkeeper, 57, M. lane
Montgomery Robert, watch and clock-
    maker, 35, Wall-street
Mulheran Richd. merchant 87, Water-st.
Morrison John, dyer, 91, Water-street
Maxwell Wm. snuff and tobacco manu-
    factorer, 4, Wall-street
Mordecai Jacob, vendue and commission-
    store, 22, Wall-street
Mount Joseph, shoemaker, 68, Cherry-st.
Merton Wm. esq. 2, Duke-street
Morgan Joseph, cutler, 27, Duke-street
Mark Phil. & Jacob, merch. 16, Dock-st·
Mecomb Jas. merchant, 28, L. Dock-st.

Moody J. tavernkeeper, 32,L. Geo.-street
Moore Wm. doctor, 15, Beekman-street
Murray,Mumford,&Bowen,merch.Cranw.
Milier, doctor, 30, Golden-hill
Myer John, merchant, 1, Fly-market
Mitchell David, earthen-ware merchant,
  27, Fly-market
Moore N. mason, Dyes-street
Mills John, shoemaker, 38, Broadway
Mills Josh. house-carpenter, 76, Broadw.
Mooney B. hatter, 43, William-street
Merritt William, tailor, 50, Wm.-street
Moses Isaac, auctioneer, 37, Dock-street
Marr J. saddler, 35, Broadway
Mennye John, school-master, 32, Gold-st.
Malcolm William, & co. 159,Water-street
M'Dougall Peter, merchant, , Q. street
M'Farlane, earthen-ware dealer,56, Wm.st.
M'Guier, tailor,24, Wm. street
M'Evers Geo. merchant, 7, Han. square
M'Lean Charles, grocer, 5, Moore-street
M'Lean John, printer, 231, Queen-street
M'Lean Mrs. midwife, 6, Broad-street
M'Leir Abraham, marchant, 19, Duke-st.
M'Lean Peter, merchant, 32, Duke-street
Maverick Peter, engraver, 3, Crown-street
M'Quin John, habit-maker, 32, Q. street

N

Norwood D. tavern-keeper, 44, John-st.
Nixon Thomas, merchant, 229, Queen-st.
Norwood R. earthenware merch. 19,Jno.st
Norton Isaac & co. grocers, 142, Water-st
Nelson William, capt. 26, Water-street
Nichols Lewis, merchant, 90, Wm.-street
Newton Joseph, builder, 2, King-street
Nitchie John, starch and hair-powder ma-
    nufacturer, 7, Garden-street
Nathan Simon, merchant, 44, Broad-street
Norden Van Luke, shopk. 3, Maiden-lane
Norris Rich. porter-house, 3, Broad-street
Neilson William, merchant, 40, Dock-st.
Neisman P. merchant, 16, Frontstreet
Nicholas W. merchant, 4, Beekman-slip,
Nicholas J. merchant, 4, Garden-street
Nash Henry & co.   , Broadway

O

Oswald Eleazer, printer, 25, Water street
Ogden Samuel, merchant, 14, Water-st.
Ogilvie Mrs. shopkeeper, 62, King-street
Ogsbur Alex. shopkeeper, 31, Smith-st.
Otterson A. tailor, 17, Hanover-square
Oudenaarde Marinus, mercht. 19,Han.sq.
Onderdonk, J. doctor, 21, Beekman-street
Ogden Lewis, esqr. mercht. 41, Dock-st.
Oothout & Dumont, merch. 13, Smith-st.

P

Powel Henry, tailor, 31, George-street
Paoeshels Leonard, tailor, 12, Geo.-street
Parker William, painter, 80, Queen-street
Pierseall & Pell, merchant, 205, Q. street
Pearssel Tho. merchant, 203, Queen-street
Prior Edmond, merchant, 195, Queen-st.
Parsons James, merchant, 194, Queen-st.
Platt Wm. paper-hanger, 61,Queen-street
Pearsall and Embree, watch and clock-
    makers, 43, Queen-street
Planton J. shopkeeper, 173, Water-street
Pattan Edward, tailor, &c. 179, Water-st
Pendleton D. merchant, 67, Water-street
Pugsley John, merchant, 84, Wm. street
Pintard John, merchant, 16, Wall-street
Phelan Joze, clergyman of the church
    of Rome, 1 Beekman-street
Pothout John, merchant 13, Smith-street
Panton Francis, merchant, 38,Wall-street
Parker Daniel, auctioneer, 23, Wall-street
Phacanon P. baker, 19, Duke-street
Postlethwait Jas. Capt. 25, Duke.street
Pierce J. esq. 14, Dock-street
Prexel J. painter, 25, Cherry-street
Philips Richard, 5, Cherry-street
Parks John, shoemaker, 10, Cherry-street
Post Jothan, butcher, 8, Cherry-street
Pexton James, carpenter, 72, Broadway

Picker, dancing-master, 1, Smith-street
Pollock Geo. merchant, 24, Water-street
Pearsse John, 37, Crown-street
Palmer John, jun. 8, Rutgers-street
Pozer Jacob, baker, 29, St. James-street
Pollock Carlile, insurance-office, 24, Wat.st.
Platt Richard, broker, 27, Water-street

Q

Quincey J. instrument-mak. 199, Water-st

R

Robinson Mrs. 14, George-street
Richardson J. merchant,   , Broadway
Risrarg Peter, tavern-keeper, 26, Geo -st.
Rickey Alexander, carman, 13, George-st.
Russel Joseph, carman, 121, Queen-street
Ronnells James, carpenter, 107, Queen-st.
Ricker Henry, cabinet-maker, 87, Q. st.
Rogers Leon. breeches-mak. 55, Broadw,
Roome Henry, merchant, 57, Broadway
Rogers & Lyde, merchants, 200, Q. street
Rogers M. merchant, 26, Queen-street
Robins Ezek. & Enoch, hatters, 31, Q. str.
Rosen G. ale & porter house, 131, Wat.st.
Rose Joseph, distiller, 135, Water-street
Rose J. hair-dresser, 141, Water-street
Rosewell J. iron-monger 174, Water-street
Roberts Michael, goldsmith, 42, Han. sq.
Rytter Daniel, tailor, 180, Water-street

Rylander Mrs. shopkeeper, 10,Wm. street
Ramage John, miniat. painter, 25, Wm.st.
Rutledge William, joiner, 214, Water-st.
Robertson Chas. shopkeeper, 83. Wm. st.
Reiley Robert, shoemaker,5,L. Queen-st.
Remsen John, merchant, 29, King-street
Robuck Jarvis, cork-cutter, 54, King-st.
Renson Wm. & co. merchts, 39,Broadst.
Rogers John Dr. minister of the united
    presbyterian congreg. 7, Nassau-street
Ritter John, tailor, 54, Nassau-street
Roy Le Jacob & Sons, merchts, 31,M.lane
Relay Henry, merchant, 30, Maiden-lane
Ritter Peter, jeweller, 51, Broadway
Richardson John, shopkeeper,30,Smith-st.
Roberts Robert, hatter, 24, Smith-street
Retson & Bayard, merch. 4, Hanover-sq.
Remsen Henry, merchant, 8, Han. square
Robertson Alex. merchant, 12, Han. squ.
Roberts M. Miss, milliner, 42, Wall-street
Ramsay John, merchant, 51, Wall-street
Rhodes Tho. boarding & lodg. 80, Wat.st.
Rierwick James, merchant, 7, Dock-street
Roseumen Richd. tinman, 37,L. Dock-st.
Rkissum Peter, merchant, 7, Peck's-slip.
Remsen W. & J. grocers, 7 Whitehall
Romaine Nicholas, 3, John-street
Renson Henry,shoemaker,32Cherry-street
Ritter Michael, goldsmith, 24, Flymarket
Resler J. tallow-chandler, 34, Broadway,

Ross Mrs. grocer, 37, Broadway
Richardson J. jeweller, 69, Broadway
Read & Bogardus, merchts. 244, Q.street
Read Jacob, merchant, 7, William-street
Roosevelt & Son, sugar-refiners, 159, Q. st.
Raydock & Warr, merchants, 49, Qu. st.
Randall Son & Stewarts, merchts. 10, H.sq.
Robertson Robert, merchant, 73, Wm.st.
Robertson Robert, merchant, 81, Wm. st.
Richards Smith, grocer, corner of Old
    Slip and Little Dock-street
Roston R. Edward, 191, Queen-street

S

Spering Henry, shoemaker, 66, Broadway
Shea George, merchant, 1, Hunter's-Quay
Sutten Kellep, shopkeeper, 8, George-st.
Shea Patrick, livery-stables, 5, George-st.
Stanton Jasper, grocer, 3, George-street
Snell Elizabeth, school-mistress, 117, Q.st.
Stestrich G. baker, 150, Queen-street
Seaton Mrs. boarding-school, 25, Smith-st.
Sutton Wm. ropemaker, 104, Smith-street
Stringham Joseph, Captain, 110, Smith-st
Snoe & Hay, shoemakers, 84, Smith-street
Shattel John, shoemaker, 93, Smith-street
Slyhum Benj. Captain, 96, Queen-street
Sebring Barlet, 28, John-street
Stevenson Hay & co. merchants,   , Q st.
Sands Stephen, clock & w. mak. 199, Q. st

Sanson, Murray & co. merchts, 182, Q.str.
Sands Joshua, merchant, 73, Queen-street
Smith T. shoemaker, 58, Queen-street
Seamen Willet, merchant, 57, Queen-str.
Stites John, merchant, 180, Queen-street
Scott & co. 44, Queen-street
Saidler James, merchant, 34, Queen-street
Service Rob. & Geo. merchants, 27, Q. st
Shotwell & Embree, merchants, 21, Q.st.
Scriba & co. merchants, 17, Queen-street
Sickles Gart. shoemaker, 166, Water-st.
Stewart R. tobacconist, 42, Hanover-sq.
Sarly & Barnwell, merchants, 193, Wat st
Salter & Chetwood, merchants, 8, Wm. st
Starr Joseph, shopkeeper, 12, Water-street
Shaw John, merchant, 213, Water-street
Smith P. Wm. apothe. 205, Water-street
Sharp Mrs. merchant, 29, Water-street
Sears & Smith, merchants, 62, Water-street
Seaman John, grocer, 66, Water-street
Stephenson Mrs. 24, Maiden-lane
Smith Jane, school-mistress, 72, King-st.
Smith R. tailor, 35, King-street
Steel Stephen, coachmaker, 81, King-street
Schermerhorn Sam. ship-chand. 13, Prin-st
Stoughton Thomas, 9, Princess-street.
Silva Roiz Joze, 1, Beekman's-street
Staples J. grocer, 5, Maiden-lane
Stewart John, shopkeeper, 51, Maiden-la.
Shrupp Henry, tavernkeeper, 20, Smith-st

Seam an John, furrier, 20, Hanover-square
Simmons John, tavern-keeper, 63, Wall-st.
Smith T. esq. 9, Wall-street
Shepherd John, merchant tailor, 21, Wall-st
Stediford G. auctioneer, 34, Wall-street
Sherred S. Painter, &c. 14, Broad street
Sickles Henry, joiner, 26, Broad-street
Simpson Solomon, 31, Broad-street
Stewart J. 4, Duke-street
Stewart Alex. merchant, 11, Duke-st.
Sidell John, tailor, 21, Duke-street
Storm & Sickles, grocers, 35, L. Dock-str
Smith & Wikoff, merchants, 7, Old-Slip
Saltonstall & Mumford merchts. 30, Bur. sl.
Saunders Tho. shipchandler, 31, Burl. slip
Shaffers D. tavernkeeper, 54, Chatham-row
Spingler Henry, grocer, 7, Chatham-row.
Stout Benj. merchant, 6, Golden-hill
Sheafe Henry, boat-builder, 47, Cherry-st.
Simmons John, ship-carpenter, 46, Ch. st.
Shelly J. chair-maker, 50, Cherry-street
Sickles M. cooper, 34, Cherry-street
Shonnard J. merchant, 29, Cherry-street
Sheafe Henry, grocer,   , Partition-street
Saunders N. Fred. shopkeeper, 42, Broadw.
Scank Abraham, grocer, 52, Broadway
Soderstrom Richd. consul of Sweden, 63, Broadway
Stewart & Jones, ship-chand. Murray's-wh.
Shaler & Sebor, merchants, 15, Duke-street

Stakes J. grocer, 49, Wm. street
Sacket Joseph, doctor 46, Wm. street
Smith Rachael Mrs. milliner, 59, Wm. st.
Singlair Hugh, grocer, 60, Wm. street
Stewart Augustus, merchant, 7, Dutch-str.
Steuart Archibald, merchant, 68, Wm. st.
Shippey Josiah & co. merchants, 43,
     Little-Dock-street
Stevenson Tho. auctioneer, 4, Murray's-w.
Sadler and Bailie, merchants, 9, Han. sq.
Shedden, Patrick, & co. merchants, 206,
     Water-street
Schuyler, surgeon, 2, Hanover-square,
Smith Elias, 5, Magazine-street
Stevens & Hubbell, merchants, 145, Wat.st
Smith Nathaniel, perfumer & comb-mak-
     er, 185, Queen-street
Stackhouse H. grocer, 16, Cherry-street

T

Teller, doctor, tavernkeeper, 24, Geo. st.
Tap William, accomptant,   , George-st.
Thompson Thomas, farrier, 141, Q. street
Teller & Vredenburgh, hatters, 146, Q. st.
Tierman Gabriel, tavernkeep. 111, Q. st.
Thompson George, butcher, 128, Q. st,
Titus Henry, lodging, &c. 30, Queen-st.
Tear John, linen draper, 54, Broadway
Taylor John, & co. 225, Queen-street
Thomas Thomas, coppersmith, 206, Q. st.

Tom Thomas, grocer, 165, Water-street
Thompson & Forbes, shopk. 176, Water-st
Turrell E. merchant, 9, Wm. street
Turner John, merchant, 17, Wm. street
Thompson Wm. captain, 28, Wm. str.
Thompson Thomas, tailor, 58, Water-st
Taylor Wm. shoemaker, 47, Maiden-lane
Thurman John, esq. 58, Cherry-street
Thomas John, house-carptr. 9, L.Queen-st
Taylor John, merchant, 23, King-street
Trent doctor, 16, Nassau-street
Telyan V. chair-maker, 2, Broad-street
Tinker Jas. Capt. 15, Little George-street
Tiflee N. Capt. 33, Cherry-street
Turrell E. merchant, 9, Maiden-lane
Tower J. grocer, 10, Cherry-street
Tillery James, doctor, 89, Broadway
Thomas William, grocer, 242, Q. street
Tuck. Daniel, & co. merchts. 3, L. Dock-st
Turner William, shoemaker, 35, Wm. st.
Thompson Alex. & John, merchants, 63,
    William-street
Turner John, jun. merchant, 79, Wm. st.

U

Varick Wm. merchant,   , Broadway
Undrey Andrew, 125, Queen-street
Usiah Burgh, shoemaker, 128, Queen-st
Ulick Wm. dancing-Master, 29, John-st
Van Rants Mrs. 55, Queen-street

E

Vandyk Francis, chocolate-mak. 48, Q. st
Ustick Wm. merchant, 33, Queen-street
Van Voorhis & Cooly, silversmiths, 27, H.sq.
VickabM' & Cummin, merchts. 18, Wm.st.
Vanderbilt Oliver, shoemaker, 4, Water-st
Underhill&Vernon, goldsmiths, 41, Smithst
Van Tuyl Andrew, 46, Smith-street
Van Horn David, 58, Smith-street
Vanley John, tailor, 12, Princess-street
Vredenburgh W John, 46, Dock-street
Vacher John, doctor, 9, Fair-street
Vanbleck Abram. doctor, Dyes-street
Van Cortlandt Mrs. 40, Broadway
Vicker M. J. merchant, 39, Maiden-lane
Ustick Wm. merchant, 33, Queen-street
Van Pell T. merchant, 41, Wm. street.
Vredenburgh, 145, Queen-street
Van Hook, sexton of the Dutch church
  8, Crown-street
Van Zandt Peter, 53, Water-street
Van Zandt Viner, auctioneer 202, Water-st
Van Zandt Tobias, chocolate-maker, 92,
Vandam Anth, merchant, 13, Nassau-st.

W.

Walker Samuel, tavernkeeper 12, Geo. st.
Warner Jas. & Chas. coackmak. Broadw.
Wandle Abram. inkeeper, 108, Queen-st
Waggonen Van H. and Sons, ironmon-
  gers, 1, Beekman-slip

Wood T. shoemaker, 32, Han. square.
Whitehouse John, spirit dealer, 181, Wat st
Waldron Daniel, 7, merchant, Wm. street
Walker Jas. & co. merchants, 20, Wall-st
Will Henry, pewterer, 3, Water street
White John merchant, 11, Water-street
Walton A. merchant, 210, Water-street
Waddington H. & J & co. merchants, 30,
corner of King and Queen-streets
Wilson Abram, merchant, 89, Wm. street
William Wm. china, glass, & earthenware
dealer 46, Maiden-lane
Wilson James, minister of the Presbyterian
church, 47, Smith-street
Wenman Richd upholsterer, 2, L.Q street
Wendover H. 11, King-street
Walsh Hugh, chandler, 50, King-street
White A. 67, King-street
Wetlock James, carpenter, 17, Princess-st
Wyley John, tailor 1, Nassau-street,
Webster G. grocer, 4, Maiden-lane
White Mrs. 50, Wall-street
Willet Taylor, grocer, 76, Water-street
Waters M. tavernkeeper 110, Wat. street
Wool J. last & heel-maker, 14, Broadst.
Webb B. Samuel, gentleman, 4, Dock-st
Wyckoff & Smith, 6, Dock-street
Woolsey George, grocer, 29, L. Dock-st
Winant Widow, tavernkeeper, 1, Moore-st
Watson James, merchant, Crane-wharf

White John, grocer, 5, Flymarket
Willement Wm. shopkeeper, 24, Broadw.
Wellse Benj. school-master, 3, L. Q.street
Wilson Thos, sail-maker, 13, Golden hill
Warrand John, merchant, 4, Dock-street
Woodhull & White, grocers, 172, Wat.st
Williams Thos. capt, 143, Water-street
Wilks J. merchant, 235, Queen-street

Y

Young John, sadler, 18, Queen-street
Youl E. cutler, 64, Water-street
Yates Richd. merchant, 28, Maiden-lane

Z

Zeller Samuel, baker, 7, Little-George-st

OMISSIONS.

Ferres John, merchant, 17, Dock-street
Fell & Graham, merhcants, 2, Crugers wh.
Osborn, boarding & lodg. 61, Water-st.
Strang Nathan, boarding and lodging
    house, 10, L. Water-street

THE HONORABLE THE MEMBERS OF

C O N G R E S S.

H IS Excellency JOHN HANCOCK, Esq.
President, Number 5, Cherry-street

Charles Thomson, Esq. Secretary, 28, K.st

New-Hamp- { Pierce Long,
shire. { Sam. Livermore. } Esqrs.

Massachu- { Rufus King,
setts { Nathaniel Gorham,
{ Nathan. Dane
{ Theod. Sedguick. } Esqrs

Rhode-
Island. {

Connecticut. { Stephen M.Mitchel,
{ William S. Johnson. } Esqs

New-York. { John Lawrence,
{ John Haring,
{ Melancton Smith,
{ Peter W. Yates. } Esqrs

New-Jersey. { LambertCadwallader
{ John CleveSymmes,
{ Josiah Hornblower. } Esq

E 3

Pennsylvania.	Charles Pettit, John Bayard, Arthur St. Clair, William Henry, James Wilson,	Eqrs.

Delaware.	John Vining, Gunning Bedford, ju.	Esqrs

Maryland.	William Hindman, John Henry, Samuel Chase,	Esqrs

Virginia.	Richard Henry Lee, James Monroe, William Grayson, Edward Carrington, Henry Lee.	Esqrs

N. Carolina.

S. Carolina.	Charles Pinckney, Jacob Read, John Bull, David Ramsay, John Kean.	Esqrs

Georgia,   William Houston, Esquire.

To be heard of at the Congress' Office, 81, Broadway, corner of King-street.

Grand Departments of the United States.

His Excellency John Jay, Esq. Secretary for foreign affairs, 8, Broadway

Henry Remsen, jun, Esqr. Secretary to do.

The Hon. Henry Knox, Esqr. Secretary at war, 15, Smith street

The Hon. Walter Livingston, Samuel Osgood, and Arthur Lee, Esqrs. Commissioners of the Treasury.

James Milligan, Esqr, Comptroller Gen.

Joseph Nourse, Esqr. Register General.

John Dier Mercier, Esqr. Auditor Gen.

John Pierce, Esqr. Pay-master General, and Commissioner of Army Accounts. 14, Dock-street

Edward Fox, Esqr. General-Hospital Department, 7, Cherry-street

William Denning, Esqr. Quarter-Master General, 18, Wall-street

Jonathan Burral, Esq. Commissary General, 22, Broadstreet

Joseph Bindon, Esqr. Clother-General, 66, William-street

Joseph Pennel, Esqr. Marine Department.

Commissioners for settling the Accounts of the Citizens of the United States who have Claims against them,

New-Hampshire,	Stephen Gorham,
Massachusetts,	Stephen Flint,
Rhode Island,	Edward Chim,
Connecticut,	Wm. Thompson,
New-York,	Wm. Barber,
New-Jersey,	Benj. Thompson,
Delaware,	Wm. Winder,
Pennsylvania,	{ Benjamin Stelle and John Story,
Virginia,	Andrew Dunscomb,
Maryland,	John White,
South-Carolina,	Gulliam Aertson,
North-Carolina,	Andrew Hindeman,
Georgia.	None.

List of the SENATE *of the State of
New-York.*

His Excellency GEORGE CLINTON,
Esqr. Governor.

Hon. Pierre Van Cortlandt, Esqr. Lieut.
Governor, and President of the Senate.

For the Southern District.

Isaac Roosevelt,
Alexander M'Dougall,
Isaac Stoutenburgh,
Stephen Ward,
Smauel Townsend,
Lewis Morris,
Ezra l'Hommedieu,
Thomas Tredwell,
William Floyd,
} Esquires.

For the Middle District.

Jacobus Swartwout,
William Allison,
Joseph Gashiere
Arthur Parks,
} Esquires.

For the Western District.

Jacob G. Klock,
Abraham Yates, jun.
Andrew Fink,
Philip Schuyler,
Peter Van Ness,
Valkert P. Dow,
} Esquires:

For the Eastern District.

John Williams, ⎫
Ebenezer Russell, ⎬ Esquires.
David Hopkins, ⎭

Abraham B. Banker, Esqr. Clerk.

LIST of the Hon. Members *of* Assembly *elected for the several Counties in the State of New-York, in April,* 1785, *for the year ensuing.*

For the City and County of New-York..

John Stagg,	Robert Boyd,
William Denning,	Isaac Sears,
William Malcom,	Robert Troup,
William Goforth,	William Duer.
Evert Bancker,	

For the City and County of Albany.

Peter Vrooman,	Leonard Bronck,
John Lansing, jun.	James Gordon,
John Taylor,	John Livingston,
Henry Glenn,	Abram.J.V.Alstyne,
Jacobus Schoonhov.	Lawr. Hogeboom,

For the County of Suffolk.

Jonathan N. Havens,	Jeffery Smith,
David Hedges,	Nathaniel Gardner,
Thomas Youngs,	

For the County of Ulster.

Nathan Smith,   Corn. Schoonmaker,
David Galatian,   Joseph Hasbrouck,
Thomas Jansen,   Johannis Snyder.

For Queen's County.

Samuel Jones,   James Townsend,
Daniel W. Kissam, Daniel Duryee.

For King's County.

John Vanderbilt,   Charles Doughty.

For Richmond County.

Joshua Mersereau,   John Dongan.

For West-Chester County.

Philip Pell, jun.   Samuel Drake,
Thomas Thomas,   Jonat. G. Tompkins
Ebenezer Lockwood Abijah Gilbert.

For the County of Orange.

Henry Wessner, 3d. John Bradner,
Nathaniel Satterly, Gilbert Cooper.

For Dutchess County.

Dirck Brinckerhoff, John D'Witt,
Lewis Duboys,   Henry Ludenton,
Matthew Patterson, Brinton Paine.
Jacob Griffin,

6

For Montgomery County.

Volkert Veeder,   James Livingston,
Abram. Van. Horne,   Abram Arndt,
John Frey,   William Harper.

For Washington County.

Albert Baker,   Ichabod Parker,
Joseph M'Cracken,   Peter B. Tierce.

---

*Officers in Chancery, Judges, Justices of
the Peace, and other civil officers.*

The Hon. Robert R. Livingston, Esqr.
  Chancellor of the state, 3, Broadway
John M'Kesson, Esq; Register, 49, M.lane
William Cock, Esqr. Deputy-Register,
  66, Wall-street

Clerks in Chancery.

Brokholst Livingston, 12, Wall-street
Morgan Lewis, 59, Maiden-lane
John Lansing and Jacob Stephen Lush,
  Esqrs. in Albany

Masters in Chancery.

Gilbert Livingston, Paughkeepsie
Jeremiah Lansing, Albany
John Broome, Esq; 6, Hanover-square.
Hon. John Jay, 8, Broad-street
Ed. Dunscomb, Esq. Exam. 82, Wat.st

Judges in the Supreme Court.

The Hon. R. Morris Esq; chief Justice,
corner Nassau and King streets,

The Hon. Robert Yates, Esq;

The Hon. John Sloss Hobart, Esq; 47,
Crown-street.

Egbert Benson, Esq; Attorney General,
Poughkeepsie, or at 22, Maiden-lane.

John M'Kesson, Esq; Clerk of theSupreme
Court, and Nisi Prisis, Oyer and Ter-
miner, and General Gaol Delivery, 49,
Maiden-lane.

Officers of the City and County of New-York.

The Hon. James Duane, Esq; Mayor, 26,
Nassau-street.

Richard Varick, Esq; Recorder, 46, Dock-st

Abraham P. Lott, Esq; Alderman,
Maiden-lane.

Benjamin Blagge, Esq; do.

John Broome, Esq; do.

William Neilson, Esq; do.

Jeremiah Wool, Esq; do. 49, Broad-street

William W. Gilbert, Esq; do.

Nicholas Bayard, Esq; do.

Marinus Willett, Esq; Sheriff, 22, Beek. st

Robert Benson, Esq; Clerk, 22, Maiden-l.

Jeremiah Wool, Esq. Corner,

F

Commissioners of Forfeitures.

Isaac Stoutenburgh, and P.VanCortlandt,
Esquires, for the southern district.
Daniel Graham, Esq; for the middle distr.·
Henry Oothoudt, Jeremiah Van Rensle-
lear, and Cristopher Yates, Esquires,
for the western district.
Alexander Webster, Esq; for the eastern
district.
John Lamb, Collector.
John Lasher, Surveyor and Searcher.
Daniel Ferguson, Land & Tide-waiter,
29, Duke-street.
John Stevens, do. , Maiden-lane.
Henry Becker, do. , Crown-street.
Henry Devour, do. , Golden-hill.
—— Terjiay, do. Golden-hill.
William Strachan, do. Greenwich-street.
William Hustin, do. Gold street
—— Scudder, do. Gold-street
——Waterman, do. Cliff-street
John Banks, do. George-street.
Stockholm, do. Cherry-street.

Lawyers, Attornies, and Notary-Publics,
&c.

John Lawrence, Esqr. 13, Wall-street
John D.Crimshier, Esq. attorney and notary-public, 17, King-street

Aaron Burr, Esqr. 10, Little Queen-street
Alexander Hamilton, Esqr. 57, Wall-st.
Brockholst Livingston, Esqr. 12, Wall-st.
Wm. S. Livingston, Esqr. 52, Wall-street
Thomas Smith, Esqr. 9, Wall-street
Wm. Cock, Esqr. 66, Wall-street
Robert Troup, Esqr. 67, Wall-street
Morgan Lewis, Esqr. 59, Maiden-lane
John Rutherfurd, 50, Broadway
George Bond, Esqr. attorney and notary-
    public, 5, William-street
William Wilcocks, , Broad-street
Richard Varick, Esqr. 46, Dock-street
James Giles, Esqr. 65, Maiden lane
John M'Kesson, Esq. 49,Maiden-lane
John Keesse, Esq. not.-pub. 227,Q.-street
Peter Ogilvie, 144, Queen-street
—— Depeyster, Esq. , Queen-street
—— Cozine, Esq. 55, Beekman-street
C. J. Rogers, Esq. 42, Beekman-street
Jacob Remsen, Esq. 55, Broad-street
John Ricker, Esq. corner of St. James-st.
John Shaw, Esq. 19, Cliff-street
Daniel C. Verplanck, Esq. 3, Wall-street
R. Morris, Esq. 1. Wall-street
Jas. M. Huges, Esq. conveyancer and no-
    tary public, 20, Wall-street
Joseph Winter, Esq. 184, Water-street
John Kelly, Esq. conveyancer, land, and
    money-broker, 56, Smith-st.

Jacob Morton, Esq. 215, Water-street

E. Dunscomb, Esq. notary-public, 182, Water-street

Dehart and Randall, 26, Water-street

Edward Antill, esq. Broadway

Richard Borner, esq.   , St. James-street

Cornelius Bogart, esq. 22, Beekman-street

Wm. Popham, esq. notary-public, K. st.

Messrs. Campbell and Cutting, esqrs.   , Wall-street

Joshua Bagrey, esq.

John Woods, esq. conveyancer and notary-public, 135, Queen-street

John H. Woodall, notary-public

Edward Livingston, esq. 51, Queen-street

—— Pell, esq. Westchester

List of the Officers of the Grand-Lodge of Free and Accepted Masons, of the State of New-York.

The Hon. Robert R. Livingston, Esquire, Grand Master for the State of New-York,

William Cock, Esq; past grand master,

Samuel Kerr Esq; deputy grand master,

The Hon. Peter W. Yates, Esq; senior grand warden,

James Saidler, Esq; junior grand warden,

Daniel M'Cormick, Esq; grand treasurer,

James Giles, Esq; grand secretary.

Officers and Directors of the Bank of New-York.

Isaac Roosevelt, Esq. President.
William Maxwell, Esq. Vice-President.

Samuel Franklin,
Nicholas Low,
Daniel M'Cormick,
Robert Bowne,
Thomas Stoughton,
Joshua Waddington, } Esqrs. Directors.
Comfort Sands,
Thomas Randall,
Alex. Hamilton,
John Vanderbilt,
James Buchanan,

William Seton, Chashier.
Charles Wilkes, Teller.
Peter Hughes, Accountant.
David Rudy, Receiver.
Michael Boyle, Runner.
William Magee Seton, Clerk of discounts.
Walter Scott, Porter.

Rules observed at Bank.

The bank is open every day in the year, except Sundays, Christmas Day, New-Year's Day, Good Friday, the 4th of July, and general Holydays appointed by legal authority. The hours of business from

E 3

ten to one o'clock in the forenoon, and from three to five in the afternoon.

Discounts are done on Tuesdays and Thursdays in every Week, and Bills or notes brought for discount, must be left at the bank on Wednesday and Saturday mornings under a seal cover, directed to *William Seton*, cashier : The rate of discount is at present fixed at Six per Cent. Per Annum ; but no discount will be made for longer than forty-five days; nor will any note or bill be discounted to pay a former one ; payment must be made in bank notes or specie. Three days of grace being allowed upon all bills and notes, the discount will be taken for the same.—Money lodged at the bank may be re-taken at pleasure, free of expence, but no draft will be paid beyond the balance of account.—Bills or notes left with the bank will be presented for acceptance, and the money collected free of expence : In case of non-payment and protest,the charge of protest must be borne by the person lodging the bill.—Payments made at the bank, must be examined at the time, as no deficiency suggested afterwards will be admitted.

Gold coin is received and paid at the bank of New-York at the following rates:

	Dwts	Gr.	Dol.	96ths
A Johannes, weighing	18		16	
A Half Johannes,	9		8	
A Spanish Doubloon,	17		15	
A Double Span. Pistole,	8	12	7	48
A Spanish Pistole,	4	6	3	72
A British Guinea,	5	6	4	64
A ditto Half Guinea,	2	15	2	32
A French Guinea,	5	4	4	52
A Moidore,	6	18	6	
A Caroline,	6	8	4	72
A Chequin,	2	4	1	78

An allowance is made on all Gold exceeding the above standard, at the rate of Three pence per grain; on all gold short of the above weight Four pence per grain is deducted.

COLUMBIA COLLEGE.

PROFESSORS.

Greek & Latin languages,—Mr. William Cochran, Ranelagh.

Geography,--Rev. John D. Gros, College.

Rhetoric and Logic,—Rev. Benj. Moore, Broadway.

Natural Philosophy and Astronomy—Dr.
  Samuel Bard, , Broad street
Mathematics—Mr. John Kemp, College.

French language,—Rev. Lewis Tetard,
German do.—Rev. John D. Gros,
Oriental do.—Rev. Dr. Kunze, 24,
  Chatham-street.

Anatomy,—Dr M'Knight,
Chemistry &Natural History,—Dr.Moyes,
Practice of Physic,—Dr.Romaine, John-st.
Midwifery,—Dr. Crosby,
Instituets, of Medicine,—Dr. Kissam.

Rector of the Grammar School,—Mr.
  William Cochran,
Assistant Teacher,—Mr. James Hardy,

The Days of examination for admission
into the College, are the first Mondays in
April, July, October and January. Public examinations of all the students begin
on the same days, at eleven o'clock A. M.
—The annual Commencement is held on
the second Tuesday in April.

The Society for promoting the Manumission of Slaves, and protecting such of them as have been, or may be liberated,— meets at the Coffee house.

The Hon. John Jay, Esq; President,
Samuel Franklin, Vice President,
John Murray, junior, Treasurer,
John Keese, Esquire, Secretary,
Willet Seaman,
William Shotwell,
Jacob Seaman,
Augustus Sydill,
Robert Troup, Esquire,
White Matlack,

} Standing Committee.

Gold and Silver Smith's Society, meets on Wednesdays, at the house of Walter Heyer.

MYER MYERS, Chairman,
Members,—Samuel Johnson,
William Gilbert, Esq;   , Broadway,
Otto De Perrizang,
William Forbes, 88, Broadway,
John Burgher, 207, Queen-street
Daniel Chene,
Cary Dunn,
Benjamin Halsted, 13, Maiden-lane
Ephraim Brasher, 1, Cherry-street.

LIST *of the Members of the Cincinnatti of the State of New-York.*

ALEXANDER M'DOUGALL, Esq; President,
Baron Stuben, Esq; Vice President,
Philip Cortlandt; Esq; Treasurer,
Richard Platt, Esq; Deputy Treasurer,
Robert Pemberton, Esq; Secretary,

George Clinton,
Samuel T. Pell,
John F. Hamtramch,
Jonathan Hallet,
Israel Smith,
Theodosius Fowler,
Henry Vanderburg,
Henry Pauling,
Samuel Dodge,
Charles Weissenfelts,
James Johnson,
B. Swartwout,
Samuel Talmage,
Daniel Denniston,
Nehemiah Carpenter
Christopher Hutton,
William Colbreath,
Goose Van Schaick,
John Gano,
Daniel Minema,
Abner Prior,
Michael Connolly,

R. Cochran,
Rod. V. Hovenberg,
Ephraim Woodruff,
Joseph Frilick,
Samuel Dodge,
B. Vanderburgh,
Henry Dubois,
Jacob Wright,
Benjamin Walker,
Wm. Stephen Smith,
P. Magee,
John Graham,
Jer. Van Ransselaer,
Aaron Aorson,
John Marsh,
Ephraim Snow,
John Fondey,
Henry Tiebout,
Willea Ryckman,
G. Lan..g,
James ...g,
R. Wilson,

John C. Ten Broeck, Henry Cunningham,
Samuel Lewis, Ebenezer Stevens,
Cornelius V. Dyke, Sebastian Bauman,
John Furman, Daniel Niven,
Charles Parsons, Peter Taulman,
Benjamin Herring, William Price,
George Sitez, John Doughty,
Cornelius J. Jansen, Isaac Smith,
Abram.Hardenburg Jacob Kemper,
Dy Fondey, Thomas Machin,
Henry V. Woert, Peter Anspach,
Jacob H. Wendell, Henry Dember,
J. Morrel, Isaac Guion,
Adam Ten Broeck, Jonas Adcamson,
Benjamin Gilbert, R. Burnet, jun.
John Elliot, Caleb Brewster,
Derik Schuyler, George Fleming,
Leonard Bleecker, Joseph Foote,
Joseph Morrel, Pierrie Regnier,
C. Sweet, Geo. J. Denniston,
William Peters, William Tapp,
John Lamb, Thomas Hunt,
Andrew Moodie, William Belknap,
Michael Wetzell, John F. Vacher,
John Shaw, Benjamin, Ledyard,
Ephraim Fenns, Charles Graham,
James Bradford, Fred. Weissenfelts,
Cornelius Swartwout John Cape,
John Reed, Elihu Marshall,
Isaac Hubbel, James Stuart,

7

Daniel Parker, jun.
James Gilliland,
Abraham Hyat,
Richard Varick,
Ranald S.M'Dougal
John Lawrence,
Simeon Dewitt,
Andrew Englis,
Jacob Reed,
George Leaycraft,
William Leaycraft,
Daniel M'Lean,
William Strachan,
Abraham Legget,
I. Stake,
James Giles,
Peter Nestle,
J. Bagley,
Samuel Hay,
John Cockran,
John Conway,
Edward Dunscomb,
John D. Crimshier,
Duncan Campbell,
Aquila Giles,
Marinus Willet,
Peter Vasborough,
Francis Hanmer,
Samuel Logan,
Peter Ganswoort,

Matthew Clarkson,
Robert Johnson,
John Waldron,
Garrit J. V. Wagener
Thos. Fred. Jackson
William W. Morris
John Smith,
John Green, capt. in
    the navy,
Thomas Tillotson,
John Bard,
Stephen Graham,
John Grier,
A. White,
Alexander Clinton,
J. Brewster,
Jonathan Lawrence,
Arthur Thompson,
Daniel Gans,
Thomas Turner,
Hen. Em. Lutterloh
John Santford,
Morgan Lewis,
David Van Horn,
Teunis V. Wagener
Silas Gray,
Charles Newkirk,
Tjerck Beckman,
Nathaniel Henry.

HONORARY MEMBERS.

Lt. Gov. Cortlandt, Colonel Floyd,
Chan. Livingston, Capt D. Williams,
Chief Justice Morris, Maj. Thomas Moffat
Judges, { Yates and H. R. Livingston,
{ Hobart, Upper Manor,
James Duane, Esq; Wm. Duer, ⎫
Judge Platt, J. Lansing, ⎬ Esqrs
General Morris, Philip Pell, ⎭
Colonel M'Laughry Dr. S. Gano.
Colonel Hathorn,

STANDING COMMITTEE.

Doctor Cockran, Colonel Antill,
Captain Dunscomb, Captain Reed,
Mr. Brooks, Major Stagg,
Colonoel Hay, Captain Guion.
General Webb,

Delegates for the General Meeting of the
Committee.

Baron De Steuben, Colonel Troup.
General Webb,

The Society, for the sake of frequent
communications, is divided into districts,
viz.—the southern and northern districts,—
the former including Long-Island, Staten-
Island. New-York-Island, the counties of
G

West-chester, and Orange ; The latter
including the rest of the State. These
districts to hold their meetings in New-
York and Albany, respectively, on the
last Monday in March, and first Monday
in November, every year.

For the Southern District.

Marinus Willet, Esquire, Chairman,
Edward Antill, Esq; Dep. Chairman,
Jacob Reed, jun. Esq; Secretary.

The Northern District has not yet made
their appointment.

---

*A LIST of the Officers and resident Mem-
bers of the* St. Andrew's Society, *of the
State of New York.*

DAVID JOHNSTON, Esq; President,
The Hon. Robert R. Livingston, Esq;
Chancellor of the State, Vice-President;
William. Maxwell,
William Malcom,
George Douglas,
John Ramsay, } Assistants.
James Saidler,
James Scott,
Reverend John Mason, Chaplain,
David Currie, Treasurer,
Adam Gilchrist, jun. Secretary.

RESIDENT MEMBERS.

Walter Buchanan,
Robert Bruce,
Andrew Browne,
Capt. James Black,
Archibald Currie,
Major Jas. Christie,
John Currie,
Capt. Henry Coupar
Col. Don. Campbell,
Malcom Campbell,
David Cation,
B. Crookshank,
Samuel Campbell,
Thomas Durie,
Robert Dunlap,
John Darrah,
Capt. John Duncan,
Robert Dunbar
Capt. James Dean,
John Donnan,
Capt. Robert Elder,
Walter Frazer,
James Grant,
David Galbreath,
Thomas Gillespie,
Doctor Gilchrist,
Graham,
Gourlay,

Alex. Hossack,
Alex. Hamilton,
Hugh Henderson,
Robert Hodge,
Patrick Hart,
Capt. Robert Hunter
Neil Jamison,
Capt. Arch. Kennedy
Samuel Kerr,
Dr. Kissam,
William Lowther,
Robert Lenox,
Tristrim Lowther,
Thomas Lawrence,
Brockh. Livingston,
Col Wm. Livingston
Philip Livingston,
Peter V B. Livingston
R. G. Livingston, ju.
Peter M'Dougall.
James M'Intosh,
Andrew Mitchell,
Wm. Maxwell, jun
Colin M'Grigor,
James H. Maxwell,
Jacob Morris,
David Mitchelson,
John Munro,

7*   G 2

Mr. John M'Lean,
Doctor Moyes,
James MilleganEsq;
Alexander M'Lean,
James Mitchell,
Daniel Nevin,
—— Ogilvie,
Francis Panton,
Alexander Perkins,
W. RutherfurdEsq;
James Renwick,
J. Rutherfurd, Esq;
Alex. Robertson,
Robert Robertson,
Charles Robertson,
Alexander Riddle,
William Robertson,
Lewis A.Scott, Esq;
William Seton,
J. Stevens,jun. Esq;
George Service,
William Shedden,

Charles Smith,
Dr. David Seath,
Joshua Sands,
Capt. Daniel Shaw,
Capt. Al. Stewart,
Hay Stevenson,
James Smith,
Geo. Turnbull,Esq;
John Thomson,
John Turner,
R. Troup, Esq;
John Taylor,
John Thomson,
Henry Troup,
James Tillery,
Robert Wilson,
William Wilson,
Rev. J. Wilson,
Gen.P.V.Cortlandt.
John Young,
Hon. P. W. Yates.

HONORARY MEMBERS.

James Stewart,
—— Crammond,
Thomas Allen,
John Inglis,
Geo. Wright,
John Smith,
Samuel Douglas,

P. Lawrence,
S. Loudon,
William Patrick,
George Reid,
James Brebner,
John Campbell,
Dr. J. Cochran,

Members of the General Society of Mechanics and Tradesmen.

Henry Becker,
Ebenezer Young,
John Young,
Garrit de Bow,
Dennis M'Ready,
William Crowlius,
Samuel Loudon,
Jacobus Brown,
Abraham P. Lott.
Thomas Ogilvie,
Jacob Arden,
John Stagg,
Christ. Duyckink,
Anthony Post,
Hugh Walsh,
Michael Tremper,
Peter Hulick,
Joseph Jadwin,
Edward Meeks,
Robert Manley,
Isaiah Wool,
Isaac Meade,

John Burger,
Garrit Harsin
Thomas Ivers,
George Harsin,
William Allen,
A. Thompson, jun.
William Smith,
John Bailey,
Robert Tout,
John Anthony,
John Shepherd,
William J. Elsworth
Robert Boyd,
Henry Wolfe,
William Hurton,
Jeremiah Wool,
Robert Hodge,
James Stuart,
George Taylor,
Samuel Atlee,
Ol. Mildeburgher.

ROBERT BOYD, Chairman,
John Burger, Deputy Chairman,
Hugh Walsh, Treasurer,
James Bingham, Secretary.

G 3

A LIST of *Members belonging to the Society of Peruke makers, Hair Dressers, &c. Held at Mr. Ketchum's, No. 22, Ann-street.*

David Barclay,	James Rose,
Michael Tremper,	Jacob Leonard,
Leonard Fisher,	Francis Leonard,
Thomas Winslow,	Isaac Jones,
Lorrant Marey,	Anthony Latour,
Richard Penny,	James Bell,
George Cork,	Jonathan Penny,
John Van Duessen,	Thomas Shepherd,
John Clits,	John Baldwin,
John Fenton,	Bernard Sohots,

DONALD M'KAY, Chairman,
James Stewart, Treasurer
Charles Ortzen, Clerk.

Arrivals and Departures of the Mails *at the* Post-office, *in* New-York.

A R R I V A L S.

From NEW-ENGLAND *and* ALBANY.
From November 1st, to May 1st.
On Wednesday and Saturday, at *seven*
o'Clock, *P. M.*
From May 1st, to November 1st.
On Tuesday, Thursday, and Saturday,
at *eight* o'Clock, *P. M.*

From the SOUTHWARD,
From November 1st, *to May* 1st.
On Sunday, and Wednesday, at *ten*
o'Clock, *A. M.*
From May 1st, *to November* 1st.
On Monday, Wednesday, and Friday,
at *nine* o'Clock, *P. M.*

DEPARTURES.
For NEW-ENGLAND *and* ALBANY.
From November 1st, *to May* 1st.
On Sunday and Wednesday, at *nine*
o'Clock, *P. M.*
From May 1st, *to November* 1st.
On Sunday, Tuesday, and Thursday,
at *ten* o'Clock, *P. M.*
For the SOUTHWARD.
From November 1st, *to May* 1st.
On Sunday and Thursday, at *two*
o'Clock, *P. M.*
From May 1st, *to November* 1st.
On Monday, Wednesday, and Friday,
at *four* o'Clock, *P. M.*

*** Letters *must be in the* Office, half an
hour *before* closing.

Further Omissions.

Lawrence Kortright, Esq: 192, Queen-st.
Gen. John Maunsell, Esq; upper end of
    Bowery lane
The Rev. Andrew Nugent, parish priest of
    New-York, 1, Hunter's Quay,
Richard Harison, Esq; C.L. 186, Water-st
Gen. Alex. M'Dougall, Esq; 8, Duke-st.
Rauld ———, 8, Duke-street
John Walkins, Esq; 8 Broadway,
Carr and ———, merchants, 215, Q.street
Goldsbrow Banyer, Esq. 56, Smith-street
Captain Thomas Bibby, 10, Smith-street,
Mr. Mechaux, at Mr. Weir's, Wall street.

To the Inhabitants of the City of New-York.

GENTLEMEN,

MR. F R A N K S returns his sincere
thanks to his Friends and the Public, for
their kind and liberal encouragement
towards his publication of the *New-
York Directory;* he humbly requests
they may indulgently excuse any errors,
inaccuracies, or omissions, which may appear, and impute them only to the local
disadvantages he laboured under, in this
first attempt; as he intends in the future

editions, he shall have the honour of annually presenting them, to have it more in his power to be exact, correct, and circumstantial; as the number of subscribers are but few (which he attributes to a want of knowledge of the utility of this production, it being the first of the kind ever attempted in this city;) he makes bold to call on the citizens at large, for every information, that they think will prove conducive to its future correctness. Their directions will be thankfully received and gratefully acknowledged by Mr. FRANKS, at his lodgings, No. 66, Broad-way, or at Mr. KOLLOCK's Printing-Office.

N. B. Mr. FRANKS has ready for *Publication*, a TREATISE of BOOK-KEEPING, digested for the inland and foreign Trade of *America.*—This Work, which he hopes will prove very useful, he would willingly submit, previous to his putting it to Press, to the inspection of the Gentlemen of the Mercantile Line, and will consider himself much honoured if they favour him with their patronage, as he intends laying it before them at their respective residences.

☞ The NEW YORK DIRECTORY, will, in future, be published every *twentieth* day of *May* in each Year.

DAVID FRANKS,

CONVEYANCER and ACCOUNTANT, No. 66, Broadway.

BEGS Leave to return his sincere thanks to his friends and the public, for their past favours, and hopes the cheapness of the following will continue him their favours:

	£.		
Drawing a Lease and Re-lease, on Parchment,	1	14	0
Ditto, ditto, ditto, on Paper,	1	8	0
Ditto, a Bond, - -	0	8	0
Ditto a Power of Attorney,	0	14	0

Mr. Franks having served a regular apprenticeship to his father, a very eminent attorney in Dublin, and having, besides, transacted business, for some years, for Counsellor Franklin of said city, he hopes, will entitle him to the countenance of the Gentlemen of the Law Department in this metropolis ; to merit whose esteem and approbation will be his particular study,— he will thankfully receive business from them on the most reasonable terms.

N. B. To prevent complaints, generally arising from employing unexperienced Clerks, Mr. Franks has lately engaged a young man from Dublin, of unexceptionable abilities.